KAMĀLAMALAMA

THE LIGHT OF KNOWLEDGE

A Hawaiian Way to Knowledge, Health, and Excellence

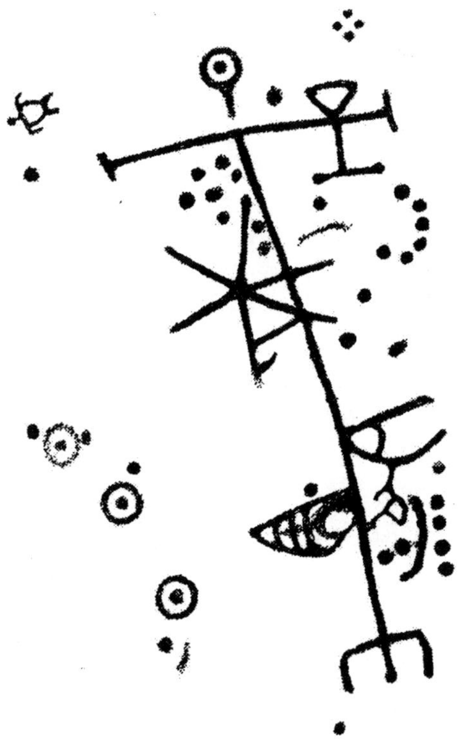

By

PATRICK KA‘ANO‘I

The title page illustration is a Lono petroglyph figure with sails from Pu'uloa, Puna, Hawai'i. See *Hawaiian Petroglyphs* by J. Halley Cox with Edward Stasack, Bishop Museum Press, Honolulu, Hawai'i, 1980.

All other graphics and illustrations are by the author.

ISBN: 978-0-9815212-0-6

Library of Congress Control Number: 2008921058

First edition

Honolulu, Hawai'i

Revised Edition

PO Box 50291
Las Vegas, Nevada 89016-0291

E-mail: Lvhalau@aol.com

Dedicated to my wife Heinke, for without her this book would not have been written

and to my mākua David Ka‘ano‘i (Ha‘o), Jr., and Emily Nunes for my life and inspiration,

and to my kūpuna David Ka‘ano‘i Ha‘o and Josephine Kalaniali‘i Ho‘opi‘i for my pride and heritage of being Hawaiian.

To you I dedicate this work, with everlasting love and aloha. Me kealoha poina ‘ole!

Patrick Ka‘ano‘i

TABLE OF CONTENTS

ABOUT THE AUTHOR

Patrick Ka'ano'i was born and raised in Hawai'i of Portuguese and Hawaiian ancestry.

He's the author of *The Need for Hawai'i* and *Birthtones–Sound & Color Rhythms* published by Ka'ano'i Productions. He is also co-author of *The Hawaiian Name Book* by Bess Press and other published articles on Hawaiian culture.

Ka'ano'i is a co-founder of Lā Hae Hawai'i–Hawaiian Flag Day July 31st and author of the amended Hawai'i revised statutes regarding the codification of The Hawaiian Flag.

As a performer, musical composer, and video producer, Patrick has also created a video titled, "The Story of the Hawaiian Flag" for Pu'ukoholā Heiau National Historic Site on the Big Island of Hawai'i.

Patrick now lives in Las Vegas, Nevada, and maintains a Web site called Halau O Ka Lama—Hawaiian Studies on the Web.

INTRODUCTION

THE LIGHT OF KNOWLEDGE

So often have I heard and felt the frustration of Hawaiians still trying to understand and find our way in Western society. The native tenure of our lands and Hawaiian way of life has mostly given in to Western systems of economics, individualism, government, land and ecological management. As unbelievable as it may seem, in Hawai'i, there is a quiet belief that white or haole blood is a preferred source of intelligence. Why? And how has the Hawaiian culture failed to maintain or excel in our place in Western society? Our cultural achievements are legendary, our oral literature rated among the world classics. What can be the root of this disparity? Is there another, underlying reason for explaining the differences between a Hawaiian and Western mind?

Recent studies have made it no mystery that each one of us has right and left brain attributes. The left side of our brain is objective, verbal and analytical while the right side of our brain is subjective, visual, and creative. Likewise, cultures can also be identified as either objective left brained or subjective right brained. Of course, it takes two sides of our brains to function, so individually and culturally we may be identified as either objective-subjective or subjective-objective depending on one's personal and/or cultural base.

It is not a matter of denying or supporting one or the other way of thinking, but rather to master the two depending on your personal and/or cultural base. The Hawaiian way of thinking is subjective while the Western mind is objective. Understand this and the vision of life unfolds.

This point of view and source of understanding all things Hawaiian, or what I call *Hawaiianology*, is founded on *Kahunaism*, Hawaiian religious-philosophy.

Please note that the *Hawaiian Dictionary* (Mary Kawena Pūku'i and Samuel H. Elbert, University of Hawaii Press, Honolulu, 1981, hereafter referred to as PE) defines a *kahuna* as a "priest, minister, sorcerer, expert in any profession." The *kahuna* would specialize in various skills and arts such as canoe building, astronomy, navigation, medicine, etc. (PE, p. 106). In addition, this book defines a *kahuna* as a Hawaiian religious-philosopher, which is what all *kahuna* must be to apply and perfect their knowledge and craft. "Philosophy" in this context stands for a system of understanding and relating to life while "religious" is defined as the hope of what is and yet to be. They are one and the same in *Kahunaism* and as a Hawaiian way of life.

The traditional way of learning *Kahunaism* is from the mouth of a *kahuna*, or Hawaiian religious-philosopher, but the way a Hawaiian *kahuna* learns his knowledge is from the source. What is that source and how do we get there are the questions and answers offered in this work, *Kamālamalama: The Light of Knowledge*, a Hawaiian way to knowledge, health, and excellence.

MY PLACE IN HAWAI'I

My mother's family came to Hawai'i from the Portuguese islands of Madeira, beginning in 1878. My father's family came to these islands over a thousand years ago from Tahiti. I was born and raised on the island of O'ahu, attended four elementary, one intermediate, three high schools, and one university while moving about the island with my family. Through all that time we were always near our grandparents and living a Hawaiian way of life.

Besides a contemporary education, we were taught a Hawaiian style of learning to E pa‘a ka waha, ho‘olohe ka pepeau, nānā me kamaka. Literally, it means to close the mouth, listen with the ear, and watch with the eye; to be silent, listen, and observe. This principle is one of the cornerstones of the Hawaiian way to knowledge, the principle of knowing how to learn.

My kūpuna, grandparents, taught me that the answers to all things are all around us and within us. All we have to do is ask the question to begin one's journey back to the spring of knowledge, truth, and enlightenment. What I would hear, see, and feel from the heaven above, the earth below and everything in between would be my teacher. Imagine being given a box of all truth and realizing that one of the greatest secrets of life is simply to open it.

As I explored American, European, Middle Eastern, and Oriental cultures, I realized the similar wisdom and world-class values contained in Hawaiian and Polynesian cultures. My quest was now to rediscover, understand and apply a Hawaiian way of thinking for our time.

A JOURNEY INTO LIGHT

Within these pages I am sharing, for the thoughtful mind and heart, a part of my journey into light. I offer this work so that we, Hawaiian and Hawaiian at heart, may better understand and see a Hawaiian way of learning, knowing and celebrating life.

The following chapters will introduce:

1. A Hawaiian way to learn.
    a. Be silent, listen, and observe.
    b. Ask the question; the answer is already yours.
    c. Go to the source.
    d. Kaona, the hidden meanings.
2. The journey to the source.

3. The source.
   a. The elements or sounds of creation.
      i. In the beginning was the sound.
   b. Where we come from.
   c. Who we are.
   d. Where we are going.
   e. No Satan.
4. Symbology.
   a. Family.
   b. Stars.
   c. Excellence.
5. Hoʻomanamana: Psycho-supplementation.
   a. Traditional approach.
   b. Contemporary application.
6. To know the truth, one must live it.
   a. Personal identity.
7. Aloha, an applied interpretation of love.
   a. A means to celebrate and perpetuate life.
   b. The excellence of physical and emotional love.

There will, inevitably, be those who are content or discontented with the answers given in this book and also those who are concerned about me rendering this information. However, it is not enough just to give the answer—remember, it must also be your quest and journey, to be your truth. One may hear the truth and one may see the truth, but to know the truth, you must live it.

TOTAL SENSORY PERCEPTION

Academics take note, this is a philosophical approach to a Hawaiian way of observing and relating to nature and man, *Kahunaism*. This concept is based on what I call *total sensory perception* (TSP), the ability of using the power of the total mind.

The historical results of applied *Kahunaism* are remarkable, as in the Hawaiian creation chant called the *Kumulipo*, acclaimed as " . . . a profound glimpse into the creative depths of the pre-European Hawaiian mind" (*Pacific Islands Monthly*, review of Beckwith, 1981, "The

Kumulipo, A Hawaiian Creation Chant"). Likewise, the application of modern day *Kahunaism* in this work may be revealing.

THE VALUE OF MYTHOLOGY

Because Hawaiians did not have a written language, great attention was and is placed in the perfection of committing word images to memory, via various mnemonic devices (memory aids) such as: oli (chants), mele (songs), proverbs, poetical sayings, hula (dance), and inoa (names). These various cultural mnemonic refinements constitute the vehicle of historical narratives or mythology.

The objective Western mind generally defines mythology as fiction while the subjective Hawaiian mind defines it as reality. The value of mythology is a very important element in the cultural understanding of the Hawaiian way of thinking. Mythology is defined as "the collective myths and legends of a particular people, usually describing the exploits of gods and heroes and often including an account of how the world or life originated" (*Funk & Wagnalls*, *Standard College Dictionary*, p. 896, hereafter referred to for all English definitions).

In the Hawaiian scheme of life, a god is man, a hereditary ancestor, at his best, the "supreme excellence" of nature. The memory of his "excellence" is recorded and visualized as kino lau, symbols, for future generations.

In relationship to other classic mythologies, Martha Beckwith comments, " . . . the poet of the Hawaiian 'genealogical, prayer chant' called the *Kumulipo*, 'Beginning in deep darkness,' or 'in the far past,' has hit upon a similar device to that employed by the Greek" (Beckwith, 1981, *The* Kumulipo, *A Hawaiian Creation Chant*, p. xii).

A mythology is also associated as an allegory or parable used to explain or illustrate a philosophic concept, as in Plato's dialogue, a device reintroduced in this work.

In addition to the traditional Hawaiian narrative styles such as story telling and mythology, and in keeping with the original Hawaiian style of thinking, this book introduces three modern writing techniques, rendered in forms as essay, thesis, and short story.

Introductions accompany each chapter and all are contemporary writing techniques of the Hawaiian way of thinking and communicating experiential truths, observations, and ideas.

Regarding diacritical marks: a macron above the vowels, Ē, Ā, Ō, Ū, and Ī has a long sound. The glottal stop or hamza (‘) has a short sound as in (oh-oh).

Hele i ka māpunapuna! Go to the source!

Patrick Ka‘ano‘i
Honolulu, Hawai‘i

Chapter One

KAMĀLAMALAMA: THE LIGHT OF KNOWLEDGE

INTRODUCTION

Kamālamalama or the light of knowledge is a story of my introduction into traditional and contemporary understanding of a Hawaiian way to learn: a Hawaiian way to knowledge, truth, and enlightenment.

The story is told within four day episodes, utilizing the traditional exchange of wisdom and knowledge from grandparent to grandchild, kupuna to mo‘opuna.

Much of the information in this story is presently available and acknowledged by scholars and students of Hawaiianology, the study of things Hawaiian. However the resource for the remaining information or kaona (hidden meanings) can be found by the principle upon which this story is founded: to learn how to learn; to go to the source and obtain the light of knowledge, truth and enlightenment.

KAMĀLAMALAMA
THE LIGHT OF KNOWLEDGE
IT IS THE FIRST DAY

"Where are we going?" asks the boy.

"To where we have come from!" replies the old man. He continues, "The light of the past is the light of the future."

The boy, filled with so many questions, brings a warm glow to the old man. "The answer to all things is given to those who ask for it, and in time you shall be given the answers to your questions my grandson, my moʻopuna."

"Who is Kāne?" the boy asks.

"Kāne is our father, creator of all mankind," answers the old man.

"Then who created the earth and the stars?" the boy queries.

The old man looks at the boy and says, "My moʻopuna, these things you mention also live; they are made of the same substances that have created all other life forms and are in order of creation, as it is written in our creation chant, the *Kumulipo*. All things live—if it were not so they would not exist. The space between two objects exists therefore it too is a living thing."

A fine misty rain is falling in the valley and the old man says, "Look at the rainbow there. It is Ka hakaʻehu o Kāne, which means the red crested helmet of Kāne."

The boy excitedly replies, "I see it. It is so beautiful."

The old man glowingly explains, "There are four major colors in the rainbow: red, yellow, green, and purple. Red and yellow are the colors of Kāne. Green is the color of fresh water and purple the color for breath. Have you seen the haka, the crested feather helmet of the aliʻi, the chiefs? They are in the colors of Kāne. You will also see these colors in their capes, their ʻahuʻula and kahilis, feather standards. They are symbols of the rainbow and of Kāne, and of the precious life which he gives to man and earth."

"Does the color of the tī and maile leaves symbolize water?" the boy asks.

"Yes!" says the old man. "The green of the tī leaf and maile is the symbolic color of water, the gift of life to the earth. It reminds us of its divine origin."

"I understand now," replies the boy, "but one other thing puzzles me." The boy hesitantly asks, "Why is the maile an opened lei?"

The old man gazing at the early evening sky replies, "The maile represents a river of stars. Look above—it is symbolic of the Milky Way. Our people call it I'a, it is the realm of Kāne."

The old man stares at the boy who is gazing into the night sky and gently announces, "Pau. We are finished for this day." The boy is so full of malama and begs for more. But the old man bids his aloha until another day.

IT IS THE DAWN OF THE SECOND DAY

"Yesterday, my kupuna, you mentioned that purple was the color for breath. What did you mean?"

The old man answers, "Kāne's gift to man is life and this gift is represented in his giving breath. Just as water gives life to the earth, breath brings life to man."

"The color that separates the night from the day is purple; the thing that separates the spirit from the man is breath."

"Speak to me of aloha," the boy continues to query.

"The gift of life to man and earth is given in Kāne's aloha. There is meaning to all things and it is kaona, the hidden meaning that speaks the truth. Hear this of the kaona of aloha. In the word aloha, we have two words: alo meaning face, and hā meaning to breathe. It is a gift of life from Kāne and is a living experience." Looking into the boy's eyes, the old man asks his mo'opuna, "Have you ever watched how your kupuna, your grandparents, express their aloha? They call out in the distance, 'Ui, eia nei!' in long breaths. Then fixing their eyes upon the other and finally embracing and touching noses and cheeks, they experience each others breath, warmth, and touch. This is Kāne's gift of life to us and our exchange of love celebrates this precious thing. This is aloha!"

Still looking into the boy's eyes, the old man detects something of concern. "What is the matter my moʻopuna?" the old man asks.

"At school, many of the kids talk bad of white-haoles. I am part haole and I don't like what they say. How may I find the Hawaiian part of me?" asks the boy.

"My moʻopuna, haole is not a race but rather a word to describe a lack of feeling. Look at its kaona: Hā means to breathe, ole means without. Haole means without breath, without love, without aloha. It is wrong to presume all foreign people are without aloha, for the gifts of Kāne are given to all men. It is their place to know and use them. The Hawaiian in you is to live this gift of aloha."

Another day has come to pass and the boy expresses his new and welcomed understanding of aloha to the old man as they part for another day.

IT IS THE THIRD DAY

The morning comes and the boy hastens into the valley to meet the old man once again.

"Who is Pele?" the boy begins. "Pele is a mother of earth. The black, freshly cooled lava is the symbolic color of new birth," the old man answers.

"I have seen white kapa cloth worn by our *kahuna* priests and akua temple images. If black is new life, what does white represent?" the boy quizzically asks. "Black, or more precisely, lipo, deep blue-black is the color of the night sky, Pō, the realm of spirits and honored ancestors. White, like the stars, represents the color of our spirit, the supreme brilliance, and is seen to represent those who are in union with it. The poe staff, pūloʻuloʻu, white kapa covered ball on a pahu stick, announces the earthly divinity of those present, just as a star is represented as an honored ancestor. There is also another sign," the old man continues. "When we see a pueo keʻokeʻo, or white owl, it is a special moment, for he is a spirit messenger!" "Auwē!" sighs the boy in wonder and then excitedly asks, "Have you seen the white pueo?" "I have," says the old man reverently, "and one day you will also!" Another day has come to an end.

IT IS THE DAWN OF THE FOURTH DAY

"Who is Laka?" the boy eagerly asks the old man. The kupuna replies, "Laka are the parents of the hula and the hula is the living expression of all that was, is, and has yet to be. Within the hula is the sound, the word and the power. It inspires the dancers to move their bodies to create a living expression of the story being told. Do you know a tree offering to Laka?" the old man asks the boy. "Yes," the boy replies. "It is a block of wood of the lama tree. The tree is very dark. Does the lama tree have anything to do with new life?" asks the boy.

The old man explains. "From the darkness comes life; the kaona is in the name lama, meaning light. It is an offering to enlighten the dancer to his performance, that he might himself be the light, the living expression of the story being told."

"Who is Kanaloa, Kū, Hina, and Lono?" the boy asks in one breath.

"They are part of a whole, of ʻI, supreme creation. Kanaloa is the companion of Kāne; Kū is the essence of man; Hina is the essence of woman; Lono is the messenger."

"What is the order of things?" inquires the boy.

The old man, patiently looking about, explains, "The answer is everywhere in nature, of which we are a part. Like a seed or ʻanoʻano that is planted in the earth and watered, it grows out of the soil into the sunlight to be nurtured by its rays, then matures with time to blossom and give birth to a new seed. This is the order of things!"

The boy then asks, "Why have our fathers traveled so far to come here to these islands?" And the old man replies, "You already have the answer. Hoʻi ka ʻoʻopu ʻai lehua i ka māpunapuna, the lehua-eating ʻoʻopu has gone back to the spring. You must be as the lehua-eating ʻoʻopu fish and go back to the spring, the source. Study the kaona of Hawaiʻi, know this and it will be your life's truth. In a cool place, look within yourself and then with your mind's eye behold the truth before you. It is time. Come with me, my moʻopuna," gently commands the old man. The boy follows and there in the center of a flowing stream the boy's kupuna places a smooth pebble to the boy's lips and says, "Take this pebble and let it pass through your being to remind you of our time together. You are with oia'i'o, or the truth." The old man embraces his mo'opuna and with aloha whispers, "Ahui hou!," till we meet again.

A TIME OF ENLIGHTENMENT

Left alone, the boy looks about him and as always there are vines of maile, kahilis of tī, flowing waters, rainbows arched in mist, and the setting of the day's sun. The boy recalls the question he asked the old man, "Why have our fathers traveled so far to come here to these islands?"

The old man had replied that he already had the answers and that he should study the kaona of the name Hawai'i.

"What is the kaona of Hawai'i?" the boy asks himself. He then reasons that *Hā is to breathe, wai is for fresh water, and 'I is supreme. Hā is the breath of life to man from Kāne. Wai is water, the life to the earth from Kāne. 'I is supreme or Kāne himself; creation.* As these thoughts race across his mind, he lifts his gaze from within to the sky above, and with his deeper understanding of things around and within himself, a surge of mālamalama, enlightenment, courses thrillingly through his young body. He realizes that *They were seeking that place where Kāne dwells, where we were created. It is our home and the place which our fathers and all mankind continues to seek.* As his mind's eye is greatly opened, a white pueo fleets before him. He knows! "It is heaven, our homeland, our Hawai'i!"

CHAPTER TWO

THE LEHUA-EATING O'OPU

INTRODUCTION

Chapter one introduced the word kaona (hidden meaning) and a Hawaiian way to reason and learn. This chapter moves to the next principle of enlightenment, that is: one must live the truth. It is not enough to hear and see the truth but one must personally journey to the source to make it his own truth.

The following story is based on a Hawaiian proverb from the book, *'Olelo No'eau: Hawaiian Proverbs & Poetical Sayings*, by Mary Kawena Pūku'i.

This proverb, from verse 1034, page 110, regards the quest for knowledge and understanding and uses the allegory of nature to illustrate the pursuit of one who is enlightened.

The freshwater 'o'opu is a bottom fish found in most streams of Hawai'i. The lehua blossom is found in the highest places of Hawai'i's forests and mountains and is symbolic of what is rare and held in high esteem. The lehua blossom is the object of the quest. The spring is the symbolic representation of the source or beginning; the place of knowledge, truth and enlightenment.

Another important element is the eating concept of Hawaiian symbolism. By eating a symbol, the meaning of the thing eaten becomes a part of the person who consumes it. In this story, the consummation of the lehua blossom by the freshwater ʻoʻopu is, in fact, the fulfillment of his quest of knowledge. A lehua-eating ʻoʻopu is one who has gone back to the spring or source of knowledge.

THE LEHUA-EATING ʻOʻOPU

Once there lived, in a mountain stream, a family of freshwater fish called *ʻoʻopu*. They spent all their life at the bottom of this stream, eating and moving about, totally content on what nature had given them.

Then, once in a rare moment, a red lehua blossom would slowly float on by, passing lazily overhead, drawing no particular attention from the fish at the bottom of the stream, except for one curious ʻoʻopu.

Looking up from the bottom of the streambed, he would think to himself, *I wonder where that flower comes from?* Turning to the other ʻoʻopu, he asks, "Do any of you know where the red lehua flower comes from?" Shaking their heads from side to side they suggest that he speak to the elder ʻoʻopu of the stream. "He might know the answer," they tell the curious ʻoʻopu.

Swimming over to the elder ʻoʻopu he asks, "Do you know where the red lehua blossom comes from?" "My son, our elders tell us that it comes from far away, from where all things are born, from the spring of life and understanding," the elder ʻoʻopu replies.

"Can I go there?" asks the ʻoʻopu. "Some like you have tried but have never returned. It would be foolish to risk your life for a legend," the elder ʻoʻopu tells the young ʻoʻopu.

Partially content at what the elder ʻoʻopu has shared, the curious ʻoʻopu returns to his companions grubbing along at the bottom of the stream.

At the sight of another lehua blossom, the curious ʻoʻopu can contain himself no longer. "I'm going to find where the lehua blossoms come from," he boldly tells his friends. At hearing this, all the ʻoʻopu laugh and one replies, "What a foolish thing to do. We have all that we need here: food, shelter, and family. What will you accomplish knowing where the lehua blossom comes from?"

Disappointed at their response, the curious 'o'opu swims away from the others and thoughtfully ponders, *How wonderful it would be just to know the answer.* Determined, he prepares for the journey.

THE JOURNEY

Early the next morning, the curious 'o'opu courageously begins his journey and his quest for the origin of the lehua blossom, passing other 'o'opu as he swims upstream, feeding on the bottom as 'o'opu do.

As he journeys further upstream, he finds fewer and fewer 'o'opu and less food to eat on the bottom of the stream. Still full of curiosity and determination, he swims on and on.

Tired, the curious 'o'opu rests for a while and scours the stream bed only to find it very clean, without a speck or morsel to eat. The water has also become much colder. Undaunted he feels he must go on.

Onward and upward he swims, pausing to rest a little more and more as his strength begins to wane. And just as though the end were near, he feels a new sensation. He feels a sense of weightlessness, a lilting feeling of effortless suspension.

Looking about, he sees that he has entered a place that he has never known. He has found the spring where pebbles dance and rocks still shine, where waters clear a sparkling place, a place like paradise. And as his weary body starts to fail, there is a sudden splash from up above. A lehua blossom has fallen near his head. With hunger posing its last request, he bites a piece of blossom red. Then with eyes wide opened, he finds his quest fulfilled and his mind as well, the place where all of life is born of light and understanding, the place where red lehua dwell.

Floating downstream, the partly eaten blossom finds its way above the place where he began. Looking up, the elder 'o'opu smiles because he knows what legend tells. "Ho'i ka 'o'opu 'ai lehua i hele i ka māpunapuna," he says. "One has been enlightened, for the lehua-eating 'o'opu has gone back to the spring."

Chapter Three

‘IGENESIS: SUPREME CREATION

INTRODUCTION

Where we come from, who we are, and where we are going are profound questions of identity that have always been asked by mankind. The Hawaiian way to answer who we are is simply to ask where do we come from?

Instead of using an abstract approach, the Hawaiian mind starts with the most obvious, the pragmatic approach. Man (kāne male and wahine female) is a child (keiki) born of woman, conceived from man and woman, their parents (mākua), descendant of their grandparents (kūpuna), honored ancestors (‘aumākua), first parents (ākua), who originate from the Supreme likeness (‘Ano‘i) of nature.

Where we are and where we are going are in the same order but in a forward perspective. Child to parent, to grandparent, to honored ancestor, to honored god-ancestor, to nature, the universe itself. To be born again in nature's time.

Our passage of life from beginning to beginning is measured in billions of years: from the beginning of time to the beginning of a new time, from the origin of the universe to the rebirth of the universe. There is no karmic debt, for a Hawaiian lives on as mana (power) of knowledge and excellence, passed to selected and hereditary descendants.

The Hawaiian's purpose in life is to celebrate nature and man, to pursue a life of excellence so that he too may become perfected, as supreme brilliance (ali'i), as an honored ancestor ('aumakua) and eventually to be honored in the highest degree as an ancestral god (akua). The memory of his "excellence" is recorded and visualized as kino lau, symbols for future generations.

Our immediate purpose on earth is simply to be honorably received in Pō (the night sky) by our honored ancestors before us. We are a combination of the best of our ancestors. To a Hawaiian, each individual is directly linked to every one of his ancestors back to the beginning of time. His identity is secured and future brilliantly defined as a star that shines in the night sky. He is a part of nature and nature is a part of him.

His memory as an honored ancestor has practical use in the earthly plane as well. By being honored as a celestial body, such as a planet, star or constellation, his passage through heaven guides and heralds the cycles of life and seasons. His being may span half the expanse of space, so that he may guide and direct his grandchildren on and over the face of the earth and sea.

The order of all living things, from the heaven above to the earth below and everything in between, follows the same evolutionary course. A beginning to a beginning.

Long before Darwin's theory of evolution, Hawaiians had observed and chronicled the passage of nature. A brilliant work that "chanted the universe," called the *Kumulipo*, a Hawaiian cosmogonic, genealogical, creation chant, revealed such an order as Darwin theorized.

This work, the *Kumulipo*, is still not completely understood today, however a cornerstone of its understanding is offered here in this chapter called 'Igenesis: Supreme Creation.

The reader will please note all sources have been included in the text for easy reference. The letters in parenthesis (PE) stand for Pūku'i/ Elbert and refer to *The Hawaiian Dictionary* by Pūku'i and Elbert, 1981 edition.

'IGENESIS: SUPREME CREATION

'Igenesis is a theory of life creation as applied by known elements of Hawaiian creation.

'Igenesis is a word of my own invention and is a contraction of the Hawaiian word 'I which means supreme (PE, p. 87) and genesis which means creation or origin. 'Igenesis is thus defined as supreme creation.

The elements or sounds of Hawaiian creation, on which this theory is based, come from chant, one of the Hawaiian cosmogonic, genealogical, creation chants called the *Kumulipo* (Beckwith, p. 190, verses 118 and 119), hereafter referred to as the "four elements of Hawaiian creation." This is in the realm of Pō or darkness, the time before Ao or light.

118. O piha-u, o piha-a
119. O piha-e, o piha-o

The four elements of creation are: Ū, Ā, Ē, and Ō. Note that a macron (an accent or stress marker) has been added over these characters. This stress marker is presently accepted as the proper component of this pronunciation. O piha or 'Opihapiha means uncomfortable fullness (PE, p. 269). Piha also means pregnant (PE, p. 300).

My translation of verses 118 and 119 can now be read as:

118. Full of ū, full of ā
119. Full of ē, full of ō

For the meaning of the four elements of creation, Ū, Ā, Ē, and Ō, a comparative study must be presented here.

Ū. 1. Breast, teat, udder (PE, p. 333).
'Ū. 1. To grunt, groan, moan, sigh, mourn, grieve, complain; grief, sorrow; an exclamation of delight or assent; to exclaim thus (PE, p. 333).
Ā. 1. Jaw, cheekbone. Fig.: to talk a lot, jabber (PE, p. 1).
'Ā. 1. Fiery, burning; fire: to burn, blaze. Fig.: to glitter or sparkle, as a gem; to burn, as with jealousy or anger (PE, p. 1).

ʻE. 1. Different, foreign, strange, peculiar, heathen (biblical) (PE, p. 33).

ʻĒʻĒ. 1. Redup. of ʻe, 1; contrary, peculiar, opposite; adversely (PE, p. 34).

Ō. 1. To answer, reply yes, agree; yes (in reply); tinkling or chime of a bell; resonance, as generated by the thumping of a gourd drum on a pad; sound of whistling (Kauai) (PE, p. 252).

From the foregoing definitions the following interpretation is advanced. The night (Pō) is:

118. Full of moaning (Ū) and burning (Ā).
119. Full of strangeness (Ē) and sound (Ō).

In the following section, I will show the relationship of these four elements of creation and the definitions as they are advanced into applicable Hawaiian words.

A GAME CALLED NĀʻŪ

In Kona, on the Big Island of Hawaiʻi, a children's game called *nāʻū* was played by prolonging the ". . . Ū sound just at sunset, believing that the sun would not set as long as they held their breath" (PE, p. 242). Nāʻū is also defined by the same reference as "sighing deeply." Here is an example of Ū applied to the word and game Nāʻū, to sigh deeply.

The application of the Nāʻū game, to detain the sun from setting, to hold it upright, can be realized in another definition of Ū given above as breast, teat, and udder. The physical characteristic of these anatomical definitions is that they all have a point and may stand erect or upright. In essence, the children in Kona were commanding the sun and its rays to stay "upright," to refrain from setting. In the book *Chanting the Universe*, John Charlot writes on p. 83, "In a chant about Kona, Kalola, a widow of Kamehameha I, mentions this game:

"The children are playing Nāʻū
"Holding back the rays of the sun."

Following the same Nā'ū model, we add the subsequent creation elements of:

Nā'ā. Covered with ashes, as a fire. Obs (PE, p. 237).
Nā'ē. 1. Easterly or windward (used in some localities only) (PE, p. 238).
Nā'ō. Spittle, phlegm, mucus; slimy (PE, p. 242).

The relationship of Nā'ū with Ū, and Nā'ā with Ā are clearly established. Nā'ō and Ō are related by the definition of Nā'ō, meaning phlegm that is discharged from the mouth and is accompanied by a sound or resonance. The relationship of Nā'ē with Ē will be defined in the next section.

The following section will show how the Hawaiian ākua, ancestral gods, relate to the four elements of creation.

AKUA AND THE FOUR ELEMENTS OF CREATION

The four major akua's or Hawaiian ancestral gods are Kāne, Kanaloa, Lono, and Kū. They are the god manifestation of the four elements of Hawaiian creation.

In the following illustration, notice that the last letter of the god names is the same letter or element of creation.

KĀN(E)
KAN(A)LO(A)
LON(O)
K(Ū)

By defining the four major Hawaiian gods and their kino lau, or bodies, their relationship to the four elements of creation becomes more clearly defined.

KĀNE AND KANALOA

In the last section, the word Na'e meant easterly or windward. A kino lau or body of Kāne is sunlight, which rises from the east.

Ē meaning strange can now be visualized by the rising of a new day, full of new, strange or foreign possibilities.

Kāne is "... a god of creation and the ancestor of chiefs and commoners; a god of sunlight, fresh water, and forests ..." (PE, p. 387).

Kanaloa, the great Kana, is companion of Kāne. His kino lau *is* represented by the squid, he'e or octopus (PE, p. 387). The word he'e also means to flee (PE, p. 59).

The companionship of these two major gods is realized in the definition of Nā'ē, easterly; the kino lau of Kāne, sunlight, along with Nā 'ā covered with ashes, 'A fiery, burning, the "fleeing" body of Kanaloa.

The gods Kāne and Kanaloa are now defined as:

Kān(e): sunlight; image of man.

Kan(a)lo(a): fleeing fiery-burning; emanating.

LONO AND KŪ

Lono is the god of clouds, winds, agriculture, sea, and fertility. He was also the god of the annual makahiki festival. The word lono means news or report (PE, p. 195). In Samoan, the word is longo (lono) and in Tongan, ongo (lono), which means report and sound (Fornanders, *The Polynesian Race, Origin and Migrations*, p. 203). Ō meaning resonance (sound) with Nā'ō, phlegm-generating sound, supports the definition of lono as sound or report.

"Kū (upright) represented male generating power ..." and "... also refers to the rising sun." Kū is best known as the god of war and his bodies are the 'ohi'a tree and 'io hawk. Kū literally means "upright" (PE, "Glossary of Hawaiian Gods," p. 389). Ū meaning breast, teat, and udder, a point of erection with Nā'ū, the game of holding the sun upright, supports the definition of Kū or upright.

The gods Lono and Kū are now defined as:

Lono: sound, report, perception.

Kū: upright, male generating power, the physical.

THE FOUR GODS DEFINED

The foregoing statements and evidence can now be abridged to read:

The four elements of creation, Ū, Ā, Ē, and Ō, are represented by the four major gods or akuas, Kū, Kanaloa, Kāne, and Lono. Representation of the four elements of creation are:

Kān(e): sunlight, image of man.

Kan(a)lo(a): fiery-burning, fleeing.

Lon(o): sound, report.

K(ū): upright, male generating power, physical.

'IGENESIS: AN APPLIED INTERPRETATION

From the aforementioned definitions, 'Igenesis can now take on an applied interpretation. Following is a listing of the four major akuas, gods, of Hawai'i with their respective *elements* of creation in parenthesis, followed by their first, second, and third applied interpretation.

Kān(e): sunlight, image of man, spirit entity.
Kan(a)lo(a): fiery-burning, fleeing, emanating spirit entity.
Lon(o): sound, report, perception.
K(ū): upright, male generating power, physical man.

The four elements of Hawaiian creation follow in the order of creation, for example: Man is first, a spirit entity, without physical form. Ē is the realm of the god, Kāne. The spirit entity "flees" or is set into motion. Ā is the realm of the god Kanaloa, the companion of Kāne. One of the kino lau, or bodies of Kanaloa is the octopus he'e, which means to flee.

The spirit entity Ē-Kāne, now emanating as Ā-Kanaloa, now enters the perception mode, Ō, which is the realm of the god Lono. Lono means the sound, the news, the messenger. The Hawaiian word hā means to breathe and is analogous to life. In Beckwith's *Hawaiian Mythology*, p. 46, we have a version by Westervilt, on the Hawaiian mythology of the creation of man: "Ku and Lono catch a spirit of the air and give Kane's figure (man) life." One of the kino lau of Lono is what floats in the air, clouds, "in the heavens, a long cloud, a short cloud a watchful cloud . . ." (PE, p. 195).

Now the spirit entity begins to be perceived as Ō or Lono, not yet earthbound and physical.

The last transformation for the spirit entity is to take a physical form. This is Ū, the realm of the god Kū. Kū means upright and one of his bodies is the ʻohiʻa lehua tree (PE, "Glossary of Hawaiian gods," p. 389). The tall and upright variety of lehua was used for carving temple images (PE, p. 184).

Finally the spirit entity goes full cycle and is manifested. As man, the spirit becomes a living thing.

KIʻI THE IMAGE

The final cycle of life, here manifested as man, contains all the god or akua elements of creation, Ē-Kāne, Ā-Kanaloa, Ō-Lono, Ū-Kū, and thus becomes ʻI, supreme.

The *Kumulipo* calls this first man Kiʻi, which also means image (Beckwith, *Hawaiian Mythology*, p. 60; PE, p. 136).

A COMPLETE CYCLE

This process of progression from spirit entity to upright man also takes on a regressive cycle: death as opposed to life. Kiʻi, the man physically demised, becomes prostrate and ceases to breathe, decays and returns, "flees" to the elements and returns to the fundamental source from which he emanated, the spirit entity. ʻIgenesis has now gone full cycle.

ʻIGENESIS AND THE BIG BANG

The foregoing scenario on the creation of life, as man, can also be analogous to all nature and the universe.

Here is an applied interpretation of ʻIgenesis as it relates to the Big Bang theory of the universe.

The present Big Bang theory of the creation of the universe, in short, maintains that the universe originated as one mass and exploded into an expanding universe.

One of the hypotheses to support this theory has to do with the brightness of stars, or why the night sky is dark. It's called the *Olbers' Paradox*. Light travels at the speed of 186,300 miles per second. If the universe was created from a Big Bang and is expanding, light traveling from these expanding celestial bodies, depending on the speed of expansion, would account for the relative consistency of brightness. Otherwise, if the stars where stationary, the combined magnitude of each star would theoretically light up the sky " . . . roughly as bright as 150,000 suns like ours" (Asimov, *Asimov on Astronomy*, p. 210).

Following is a comparative table of the 'Igenesis theory and the Big Bang theory of the expanding universe.

Ē-Kāne: Spirit entity; compressed universal mass.
Ā-Kanaloa: To emanate from the Spirit entity; expanding universal mass.
Ō-Lono: Perception; atomic vibration, sound to light itself.
Ū-Kū: Life; the physical entity of the physical universe, extant.

As in our former example of 'Igenesis, man became a supreme image, K'i, who progressed from its spirit entity, became a living man, regressed, and became once again a spirit entity. So too, according to the Big Bang theory, will the physical universe as we know it regress and "flee" into its original compressed universal mass and the cycle continues again.

CLOSING OBSERVATION

While being enlightened on this thesis, I couldn't help reflect on the similarity of Judeo-Christian tradition and writing. With respect may I draw these observations?

In The Gospel According to St. John in the New Testament, King James version, Chapter 1:1, 14 is written:

"In the beginning was the Word, and the Word was with God, and the Word was God."

"And the Word was made flesh and dwelt among us (and we beheld his glory, the glory as of the only begotten of the Father), full of grace and truth."

By simplifying the definition of "Word" as Sound, the two verses would read:

"In the beginning was the *Sound*, and the *Sound* was with God, and the *Sound* was God. . . . And the *Sound* was made flesh and dwelt among us (and we beheld his glory, the glory as of the only begotten of the Father), full of grace and truth."

The similarity is remarkable between this scripture and the Hawaiian Kāne, the parent image or father, originating as the creative element or sound of creation that becomes flesh in the image of Kāne, the man child of the father Kāne.

The Christian trinity of the Godhead also draws a remarkable symbolic resemblance to Hawaiian cosmology.

God the Father: Kāne the Father
God the Son: Lono the messenger with good news
God the Holy Spirit: Kanaloa the emanating spirit

In the Hawaiian pantheon, notice the absence of negative symbology. There is no Satan in the Hawaiian order of life. All men are accountable for their deeds and deeds accounted to their lives.

The final product of God is man, who is represented as Adam the first man, made in the image of God, the Father. Likewise the final product of god Kne is kne, the man, who is personified as K, the upright image (ki'i) of mankind.

Finally, just as the Hebrew language is personified in sacred text, so are the elements or sounds of Hawaiian creation personified in the Hawaiian language and chant. The parallels are striking and intriguing, and possibly a testament to the universality of man.

Chapter Four

FAMILY, STARS, AND EXCELLENCE

The quality of all life, as referred to in ʻIgenesis, is founded on excellence, or what is supreme. The Hawaiian word for what is supreme is ʻi. The Hawaiian word for excellence is maikaʻi. Notice that maikaʻi ends with the letter ʻi, denoting the quality of what is supreme.

When an Hawaiian responds to the question, "how are you?" and answers with the word "maikaʻi," which means "I am excellent," he means it sincerely. If he is not, he will so specify by saying, "I'm tired," "I'm sick," or "I'm the same as before."

To give a response of excellence, it must be a true condition of one or all of the four parts of our being:

1. Spiritual.
2. Mental.
3. Emotional.
4. Physical.

When a person lives his life in the pursuit of excellence he acquires mana, divine power. Mana can be ingested (see the chapter on "Hoʻomanamana: Psycho-Supplementation"), inherited genetically, passed on from one person to another and/or developed in the attainment of excellence. "Kings viewed mana as a genetic inheritance from god to king to king's descendant . . . the mana that made him an expert in an art or craft passed directly to one particular person, not to the family in general" (Pūku'i, Haertig, and Lee, *Nānā I Ke Kumu [Look to the Source]*, Vol. I, 1979, p. 150–151).

The amount of excellence acquired, developed, and perceived as mana or power, in one's lifetime, secures his place to be received in Pō, the spirit realm, as an honored ancestor, 'aumakua (family god), or akua (chiefly god). The attainment of perfection may even be acquired in one's lifetime and he may be so honored as an ali'i god. "Texts clearly establish that the highest ranking ali'i have qualities considered divine even before they are totally divinized after their death" (Valerio Valeri, *Kingship and Sacrifice*, 1985, p. 144).

The concept of a god in Hawaiian is not the same as in the Judeo-Christian definition. A Hawaiian god can die physically and it is his accomplishments and quality of excellence, manifested as mana, that are the miraculous and divine. An akua (chiefly god) lives on after physical death as an image, empowered, ho'omanamana, to evoke his mana to new generations. His image, or kino lau, "forms taken by a supernatural body . . . " may be a sculpture, natural phenomena, plant, animal, and/or celestial god (PE, p. 141).

The stars themselves are considered living entities of new and honored spirits. A famous constellation called *the Pleiades* that rises soon after sunset in the autumn is named after "a chief of Waimea, Kauai, father-in-law of Mano-ka-lani-po, and famous as an agriculturalist" (PE, p. 393). Even the great chief and first king of all Hawai'i, Kamehameha I, the lonely one, is associated with a very famous celestial body called *Comet Halley* (Steiger, *Comet Halley Handbook*, 1985, p. 6–7).

The celestial representation of a living chiefly god is also believed to be represented as a pulo'ulo'u, "A tapa cloth-covered ball on a stick (pahu) carried before a chief as insignia of taboo" (PE, p. 326). Although the symbolism of the pulo'ulo'u is not certain, "we know, however, that stars are compared to balls covered with tapa" (Lili'uokalani, 1978, p. 70; Beckwith 1951, p, 120–21, 125). Perhaps, then, the pulo'ulo'u represent the akua as stars, and thus in their transcendent dimension, as "spherical" or "autonomous" (Valerio Valeri, *Kingship and Sacrifice*, 1985, p. 152)

Are there other examples of honored ancestors represented as stars?

LONO-I-KA-MAKAHIKI

A very popular akua-god of Hawai'i is Lono-i-ka-makahiki, the god of the fall harvest, associated with rain, fertility, and agriculture. "A divine child, a sacred chief, Lono-i-ka-makahiki, is the cosmos described. It is his origin that begins in the deep darkness of the spirit world, in the intense darkness of the fruitful night of the Pleiades" (Beckwith, *The* Kumulipo, *A Hawaiian Creation Chant,* 1981, p. xiii). Such a divine figure would surely be represented as a celestial manifestation.

Following is an exercise founded on such a premise, based on visual symbolism supported by references and illustrations.

Lono-i-ka-makahiki is "the god of the annual fall harvest makahiki circuit of the islands when taxes were collected. He was symbolized by a tapa cloth banner suspended on a mast with a tiny carving of a human head at the top" (PE, p. 392).

Lono-i-ka-makahiki originates as a god who descends from heaven walking on a rainbow. His image depicts four distinctive and uniform facial features of all Lono images including the major Lono god of 'Igenesis. (See Fig. 1.) They are:

1. Smooth rounded head.
2. Rounded eyes with small pupils.
3. A pug nose.
4. A very large smile.

We do know that the beginning of the makahiki festival is begun at the rising of the Pleiades in the east, soon after sunset in autumn. Astronomically, it rises just at sunset on November 18th.

However, because of twilight, it would only be visible to the eye approximately an hour after rising (total darkness). Presently, this date is set at around November 2nd.

We presently have a listing of Hawaiian star names, however, only some stars are identified with these names. With the presently known stars and possible identification, along with what we know of the god Lono-i-ka-makahiki, is it possible to propose that an image of Lono-i-ka-makahiki is represented in the night sky?

Figure 1. Lono-i-ka-makahiki Festival by John Webber (Hawai'i State Archives) and a close-up rendering by the author of the top of the Lono staff to the left.

If Lono-i-ka-makahiki is an akua-god, there should be a star representation of him. If so, where and how is he represented?

The journey to the source requires revealing the known data.

1. The Pleiades is called *Makali'i.*
2. Maka means eyes and li'i means little.

If we were to suppose the little eyes to be of Lono-i-ka-makahiki rising in the east then could there also be represented other features of his face, such as his mouth and nose?

Following is a listing from the *Hawaiian Dictionary* giving possible known Hawaiian star names and their present day equivalents:

1. Hikialoalo: zenith, location directly over head.
2. Nānā-mua: Castor
3. Nānā-hope: Pollux
4. Hōkū-le'a: Arcturus

5. Kauamea: Corona Borealis
6. Makali'i: the Pleiades

All the stars listed are observed from the island of O'ahu at 21 degrees 15 minutes latitude by 158 degrees longitude. The astronomical data were confirmed by both computer and physical observation over a one-year cycle.

By translating the Hawaiian star names we get these results:

1. Hikialoalo: zenith, approaching face.
   a. hiki: arrive, approach, appear.
   b. alo: front, face, presence.
   c. aloalo: native white hibiscus.
2. Nānā-mua: look forward.
   a. nānā: to look.
   b. mua: front, forward.
3. Nānā-hope: look backward.
   a. nānā: to look.
   b. hope: behind, backward.
4. Hōkū-le'a: happy star.
   a. hōkū: star
   b. le'a: happy
5. Makali'i: little eye.
   a. maka: eye
   b. li'i: little

The stars Castor-Nānāmua and Pollux-Nānāhope are part of the constellation called *Gemini-Namāhoe*, the twins (PE, p. 240). "Although the constellation name Gemini is Roman, even the Sumerians of 4,000 BC envisioned a pair of brotherly twins in these two stars" (*Astronomy*, February 1988, p. 53). These stars, just 4 1/2 degrees apart, were also to the Chinese the embodiment of " . . . the yin-yang duality of nature," and to the Egyptians the mythical hawk-headed god of the sun "Horus rising and Horus setting" (ibid., p. 53).

I find the universal identification of the twins Gemini and Namāhoe by the ancients and in Hawai'i very fascinating. The Egyptian association of Castor and Pollux rising and setting is remarkably similar to the Hawaiian definition of looking forward (rising) and looking backward (setting). According to Johnson and Mahelona, "probably the qualifying terms -mua and -hope with mahoe- may apply to the time of rising, preceding or following as the stars rise from the east to west" (Johnson, Mahelona, *Nā Inoa Hōkū, A Catalogue of Hawaiian and Pacific Star Names*, 1975, p. 15). The star Castor precedes Pollux rising in the east.

Following the directions of the star translations as Castor-Nānāmua reaches its meridian overhead, we read:

Hikialoalo—directly overhead an approaching face, Nānāmua—look forward to the rising star, Hōkū-le'a—the happy star.

As Castor-Nānāmua passes overhead, Arcturus, presently identified as possibly the star Hōkūle'a—the happy star, rises in the east (PE, p. 71). Arcturus is followed by a crescent shaped constellation called *Corona Borealis*, presently identified as possibly the star Kauamea (PE, p. 124). (See Fig. 2.)

As these stars make their six-month trek from east to west, Arcturus passes directly overhead, followed closely by Corona Borealis. The constellation Corona Borealis begins to turn from right to left and settles in the west as the Pleiades-Makali'i (the little eyes) rises in the east one hour after sunset (total darkness) about November 2nd; the little eyes to the east and Corona Borealis in the west. If you have ever seen this with your own eyes, it wouldn't take much imagination to realize the constellation Corona Borealis is curved like a happy face. Here we have a smiling face in the west and little eyes in the east. Do you get the picture? (See the Fig. 2.)

There is a happy star that seems to be represented by a human gesture, a smiling face. However it is identified presently as Kauamea or Corona Borealis. What does Kauamea mean?

1. Ka ua mea: cause.
2. ka ua: the rain.
3. mea: thing, person, reddish-brown, as muddy water.

Although no clear translation can be rendered, the star Arcturus, presently called *Hōkū-le'a* is classed as a K2 III "cool red giant" visible

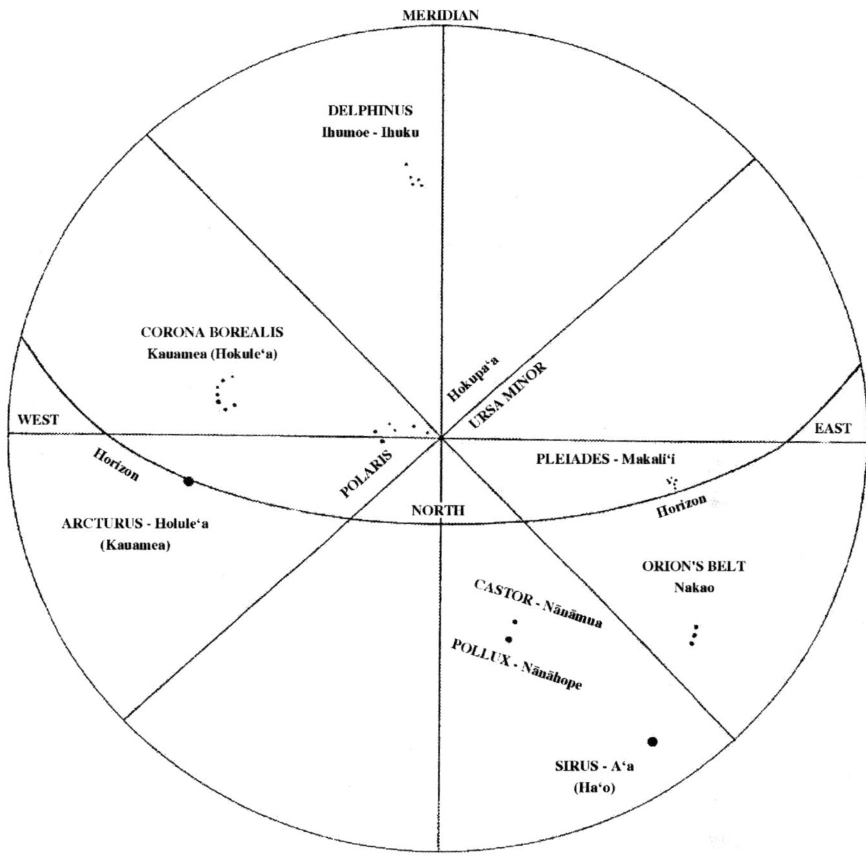

Figure 2. November-Makahiki.

to the naked eye (Menzel and Pasachoff, *A Field Guide to the Stars and Planets*, 1983, p. 262).

It seems that Kauamea and Hōkūle'a may be misidentified. Kauamea should be Arcturus and Hōkūle'a should be Corona Borealis.

When Makali'i rises in the east, Arcturus is setting in the west.

It is at this time of the year, in the autumn, one may better appreciate the vision of our hypothesis. The "happy face" Hōkū-le'a, now identified as Corona Borealis, appears in the west, while the little eyes, Makali'i, the Pleiades appears in the east. Could this be the face of

Lono-i-ka-makahiki, his smiling face, a distinctive characteristic of Lono, in the west, and his eyes in the east?

If this is the facial image of Lono, then could there possibly be another obvious feature such as a nose somewhere in between the smile and the eyes?

By studying the known list of Hawaiian stars, we have two listings: Ihu-ku and Ihu-moe (PE, p. 89).

1. Ihu-ku: rising nose (pug nose).
   a. ihu: nose
   b. ku: to rise
2. Ihu-moe: sleeping nose.
   a. ihu: nose
   b. moe: to sleep

Johnson and Mahelona refer to these stars as "a star; probably a general term for any guiding star standing (ku) above the bow (ihu) of a canoe" looking forward (Johnson, Mahelona, 1975, *Nā Inoa Hōkū, A Catalogue of Hawaiian and Pacific Star Names*, p. 7).

Possibly, somewhere, between the smile and eyes of Lono is a nose, rising from the east and in transition to sleeping in the west. Where is it?

Following within the approximate path of the other stars there is a star constellation that may be the answer. The diamond shaped constellation called *Delphinus*. (See Fig. 2.)

It has taken six months "looking forward" for Delphinus to reach its meridian after sunset. We have followed the directive of the star Castor-Nānāmua to "look forward" but what of the star Pollux-Nānāhope, to "look backward?"

From the book by David Malo, *Hawaiian Antiquities*, translator Nathaniel B. Emerson notes the subjective nature of Hawaiian interpretations: "There were considerable differences in the nomenclature of the months and divisions of the year of the Hawaiian people" (David Malo, *Hawaiian Antiquities*, 1980, p. 33).

One such interpretation is given by " . . . a Hawaiian well-skilled in the ancient lore of his country (Kaunamano)." He gives the name Māhoe-mua for the month of April and Māhoe-hope for May (ibid., p. 35). Māhoe means twin and, according to Johnson and Mahelona,

Māhoe-mua and Māhoe-hope refer to the twins Castor and Pollux (Johnson Mahelona, *Nā Inoa Hōkū, A Catalogue of Hawaiian and Pacific Star Names*, 1975, p. 15).

This directive suggests that the six months for Māhoe-mua is from May to October, "looking forward" toward the east and Māhoe-hope is from November to April. This information precisely coincides with our system that began with the stars Castor and Pollux, the twins Namāhoe, at its meridian between April and May.

We left off with the Pleaides-Makali'i (the little eyes) rising in the east an hour after sunset (total darkness) about November 2nd. A star directive is necessary at this juncture to tell us when to "look backward." I suggest the constellation Delphinus, because of its distinctive shape, latitude, and because it happens to be at its meridian at this time of the year. (See Fig. 2.)

As previously suggested, the interpretation of Ihu-ku and Ihu-moe as the constellation Delphinus now takes on a very applicable interpretation: Ihu-ku, the standing or rising nose from the east, and Ihu-moe, the sleeping or laying down nose into the west. So when Delphinus is rising to its meridian, we are still "looking forward." As it passes its meridian, we are directed to "look backward" and watch it "sleep" in the west.

For the next six months, Māhoe-hope, from November to April, we are directed to look backward, after the rising of the Pleiades-Makali'i (the little eyes), to see the setting of Corona Borealis-Hōkūle'a (the happy star), followed by Delphinus now Ihu-moe, the sleeping nose (after passing its meridian) then finally back to Castor-Nānāmua (look forward), overhead once again. The image of Lono-i-ka-makahiki is complete.

CONCLUSION TO FAMILY, STARS, AND EXCELLENCE

This whole exercise, although subjective, has been advanced to illustrate the Hawaiian way of seeing and understanding the relationship between nature and man.

A person's life is measured in excellence, mana, then empowered in his name and/or image as a star or constellation shining in the heavens, immortalized as a functional parental ideal for generations to come. Just as Lono-i-ka-makahiki has been remembered in the stars, so too are other souls remembered as the best of our family.

For my family, he is Ha'o, or Ka'ano'i-the beloved. Although no written record has the precise location of the star called *Ha'o* (see PE, p. 54), we do have a tradition recorded in our name. Ha'o means to long for, desire, to miss (ibid., p. 54). Ka'ano'i means loving heart as translated by my father and beloved for the word 'ano'i (PE, p. 24). 'Ano means kind, nature, character, type, likeness, resemblance, image, color, moral quality (ibid., p. 24). The Hawaiian word 'I, as previously defined, means supreme. Ka'ano'i literally means the supreme image or likeness. One can see why such a characteristic would be sought after or beloved.

The name of my Hawaiian grandfather was David Ka'ano'i Ha'o. All three names, including the Hebrew name David, are translated to mean beloved (Ka'ano'i, Snakenberg, *The Hawaiian Name Book*, 1988, p. 4). This was no coincidence.

The giving of any name is a very thoughtful one in Hawaiian culture. An ancestral name, such as Ha'o, is given only to a descendant of a particular genealogical line believed to possess the characteristic or inherited mana (divine power) of one immortalized as having had such a quality, such as an akua or aumakua (ancestral god). Can the stars point to a place and origin of our first ancestor called *The Beloved Ha'o?*

The star Sirius happens to pass over, at its zenith, the Tuamotu Archipelago of French Polynesia just as Arcturus passes over, at its zenith, the Hawaiian Islands.

Is it a coincidence that within the Tuamotu islands there is an island called *Ha'o?*

The star Sirius that is pointed to by Orion's belt-Nakao-the darts (of Lono-i-ka-maka-hiki), a symbol of fertility, is the seed, 'A'ā-burning bright, the "supreme likeness," the beloved desired by all. (See Fig. 3.)

The star Sirius called *'A'ā-burning bright* is a star represented in my family as "that which is most desired, the supreme image or likeness of one so beloved." This was the characteristic desired of all chiefs and immortalized as the one in our family called *Ha'o*.

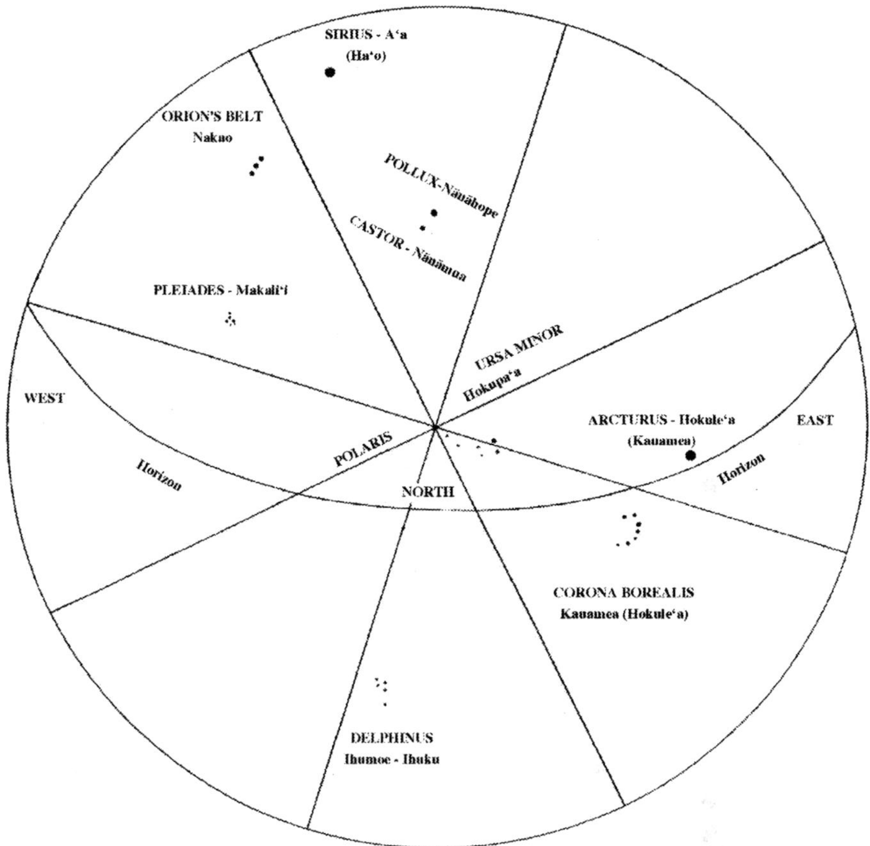

Figure 3. April/May-Namāhoe.

Our ancestral name and ideal has been remembered in chant, story, place name (Kawai-a-ha'o), island, and star. We know who we are, where we come from, and where we are going.

My father David Ka'ano'i (Ha'o), Jr., was born under the star Sirius-'A'ā-burning bright and to us he is remembered by the "excellence" of his love, shining in the night, as were his ancestors before him. So even today the power of one's mana, burning bright, is carried on and beloved by those who would remember and know its meaning.

Chapter Five

HO'OMANAMANA: PSYCHO-SUPPLEMENTATION

Chapter two introduced the journey to the source. It also featured an eating aspect or consuming of the truth desired.

In the case of the 'o'opu fish, not only did he find the answer or truth of his quest by discovering the origin of the lehua blossom, he actually ate a part of the truth, the lehua blossom itself.

The act of eating a symbol, of the thing or thought desired, is not just allegory but an actual part of a Hawaiian system called *ho'omanamana*. It means "to impart mana, as to idols or objects" (PE, p. 218). Mana means "supernatural or divine power" (PE, p. 217).

This chapter specifically focuses on the eating aspect of ho'omanamana or what I call *psycho-supplementation*. Where the seat of mana and knowledge is, how we empower it, and how we may use the knowledge today are all the subjects of this chapter.

To understand the process of psycho-supplementation, we will study two traditional accounts: a ceremony for the launching of a canoe and an account by David Malo of "the great feast" temple ceremony. Following is a traditional account of launching a canoe. It is called *Lolo'ana I Ka wa'a* or imparting brains to the canoe.

After the completion of a canoe, some traditions require ceremonially bathing it with saltwater for forty days.

After the forty days, it is readied for launching by preparing a feast on the beach while the canoe is decorated with forest greens, ti, fern and maile vines. "Then the *kahuna*, with a coconut shell filled with seawater, sprinkles the canoe, praying 'E ka'i, e alaka'i, e ho'ona'auao, e ho'olanakila, a pae ka wa'a i ke kula me ka lanakila.' 'Guard, guide, instruct, give success, until the canoe lands on the plain of the seashore with victory'" (June Gutmanis, *Na Pule Kahiko*, 1983, p. 79).

The *kahuna* then drinks a mouthful of water, pouring the remainder at the bow of the canoe and proceeds to accept, as an offering, the baked "pig's snout, tail, and four feet, a piece of meat, a red fish, a banana, and a piece of 'awa" (ibid., p. 79). From the same book, Gutmanis offers the following pule, the prayer that follows the offering (glottal stops were added for clarity).

E Mokuhali'i, Kupa'aike'e, Lea
Eia ka pua'a,
He uku, he makana, he 'alana,
He mohai 'ia 'oukou.
Ua pa'a ka wa'a (inoa) ('ano)
A e ho'olana 'ia aku ana i ke kai
O kana i'a e huli ai i ka loa'a a me ka waiwai.
E nana pono loa 'oukou
E maka'ala i na puko'a, na pu'upohaku o kahi laupapa
Na nalu, na 'ale o ka moana.
Ho'oholo no 'oukou i ka wa'a ma kahi hohonu o ke kai,
I hele ai ka wa'a a nalukai
A 'apulu, a ulu ka limu pakaiea, a kaniko'oko'o.
'Amama, ua noa.

O Mokuhali'i, Kupa'aike'e, Lea
Here is the pig,
A payment, a gift, an offering,
A sacrifice to all of you.
The canoe (name) is completed,

A (type of canoe) floating in the sea.
It is his fish to seek, to obtain wealth.
Look very closely, all of you.
Beware of the coral heads, the stone hills of the reef,
The waves, the billows of the ocean.
All of you direct the canoe to places of deep sea
That the canoe goes over the waves of the sea.
That the canoe may go till weather-worn, till worn out, and covered with limu and the cane sounds.
'Amama. It is free of taboo.

(Anonymous, referenced by Gutmanis, Kelsey translation.)

When the prayer is ended, the feast begins until all are full. Then the leftover food is gathered together in a coconut basket that includes a rock from the imu, underground oven, and that is taken out to sea with the canoe. The basket is placed in the ocean as an offering and the canoe returns to shore for the following prayer.

O kuwa o ka lani, o kuwa o ka honua,
O kuwa o ka mauna, o kuwa o ka moana,
O kuwa o ka po, o kuwa o ke ao,
O Malualani ke kuwa, o Maluahopu ke kuwa,
Aia no ia koi la ke kuwa.
Ka wa'a nei o ka luahine makua.
Ka luahine! Owai?
O ka luahine o Papa, wahine a Wakea.
Nana i kuwa, nana i hainu,
Nana i hele, nana i ae,
Nana i hoonoanoa.
Noa ke kuwa o ka waa o Wakea.
O ka waa nei o ka luahine makua.
Ka luahine! Owai?
Ka luahine o Lea, wahine o Moku-hali
Nana i kuwa, nana i hainu.
Nana i hele, nana i ae;
Nana i hoonoanoa.

Noa ke kuwa o ka wao o Mokuhalii.
Hinu helelei aku, Hinu helele mai.
He miki oe Kane;
He miki oe Kanaloa.
O kanaloa hea oe?
O Kanaloa inu awa.
Mai Kahiki ka awa,
Mai Upolu ka awa,
Mai Wawau ka awa.
E hano awa hua,
E hano awa puaka.
Hapa i ke akua i laau wai la!
Amama, ua noa.
Lele wale aku la.

Uplifter of the heavens, uplifter of the earth,
Uplifter of the mountains, uplifter of the ocean,
Who has appointed the night, appointed the day,
Malualani is the kuwa and Maluahopu,
That ax also is a kuwa.
This is the ax of our venerable ancestral dame.
Venerable dame! What dame?
Dame Papa, the wife of Wakea.
She set apart and consecrated, she turned the tree about,
She impelled it, she guided it,
She lifted the taboo from it.
Gone is the taboo from the canoe of Wakea.
The canoe this of our ancestral dame.
Ancestral dame! What dame?
Dame Lea, wife of Koku-hali‘i.
She initiated, she pointed the canoe,
She started it, she guided it;
She lifted the taboo from it.
Lifted was the taboo from the canoe of Mokuhali‘i.
Fat dripping here,
Fat dripping there.
Active art thou Kane;

Active art thou Kanaloa.
What Kanaloa art thou?
Kanaloa the awa drinker.
Awa from Tahiti,
Awa from Upolu,
Awa from Wawau.
Bottle up the frothy awa,
Bottle up the well-strained awa.
Praise be to the God in the highest heaven (laau)!
The taboo is lifted, removed.

It flies away.
(Malo, 1951, p. 129–130, referenced by Gutmanis.)

The final part of the dedication is for the perfection of the ceremony. The *kahuna* asks the owner of the canoe, "How is this service of ours?" If the ceremony was perfect in the mind of the owner of the canoe, he replies, "Maika'i!" or "Our service is good!" With that response, the *kahuna* ends the ceremony by saying, "You will travel inside of this canoe with safety because it is good." *Maika'i!*

Another example of the value of the word *Maika'i* or excellent, as used in Hawaiian ceremony, is recounted by Malo in the dedication of a luakini heiau or human sacrifice temple:

> 105. When the pigs were baked, a forequarter of each pig was set apart for the *kahuna*, which piece was termed *hainaki*. Bundles of pai-ai were also set apart for the *kahuna*, that having been the custom from the most ancient times.
>
> 106. When the chiefs and the people had finished feasting on the pork, the king made an offering to his gods of 400 pigs, 400 bushels of bananas, 400 coconuts, 400 red fish, and 400 pieces of oloa cloth; he also offered a sacrifice of human bodies on the lele.
>
> 107. Before doing this, however, the hair and bristles of the pigs were gathered up and burned and the offal removed; then all the offerings were collected in that part of the court about the lele which was laid with pebbles, after which the offerings were piled upon the lele.

> 108. Then the ka-papa-ulua priest . . . entered the lana-muu-mamao with the *ulua* (this might be the fish, ulua, or it might be the man whom the priest had killed in its stead, as previously stated) and recited an aha which was of a different rite but belonged to his special service. When he had concluded his service, he put to the king the question, "How was our aha?" [T]he king answered, "It was excellent." "Most excellent indeed," said the priest to the king; "the hook did not break; your government is confirmed." [T]hen the ulua was laid as an offering upon the lele, and the *kahuna* went his way."
> (Malo, *Hawaiian Antiquities*, 1980, p. 173–174.)

In both accounts, note the comparison of feasting on food offerings by the participants of the ceremony, the food gifts to the *kahuna* and the inquiry and confirmation of the "excellence" of the service as petitioned by the *kahuna* to the recipient.

THE SEAT OF MANA

Mana means divine power and ho'omanamana means to impart mana as to idols or objects. The foregoing examples are of ho'omanamana, the imparting of divine power to the canoe, in our first example, and to the king or ali'i in the second. The manner in which this is accomplished is when "the greater part of the offering is generally consumed by the sacrificers; and that in this manner they are supposed to absorb divine mana" (Valerio Valeri, *Kingship and Sacrifice*, p. 56).

Is absorbing divine mana and intelligence the same?

The name of our first ceremony is *Lolo'ana i ka wa'a,* to impart brains or intelligence to the canoe. The Western mind associates intelligence with the brain but the Hawaiian mind associates intelligence with the na'au, the intestines. "Traditionally, the intellect and emotions were thought to exist in the intestinal regions. (The head was the dwelling place for spirits, especially beneficent ones such as the aumākua or family gods)" (Pūku'i, Haertig, and Lee, *Nānā I Ke Kumu* [*Look to the Source*], Vol. I, p. 155).

This indicates that the divine is associated with the head while the intellect is associated with the intestines. Both are empowered, ho'omanamana, by the consuming of food offerings.

"Dancers who eat offerings consecrated to the goddess Laka ('eat to the Laka')", who preside over the hula, obtain "good knowledge and expertness to dance well," while those who "refuse to do this, will not become accomplished in the art" (*Missionary Herald*, July 1822, p. 207; referenced by Valerio Valeri, *Kingship and Sacrifice*, p. 58–59).

SYMBOLISM AND PSYCHO-SUPPLEMENTATION

The systematic naming of all things in Hawai'i, between man and nature, was a very well-thought-out process, for within the name was the image of the thing desired. For example, he'e is the name for the octopus or squid; it also means to flee. Ceremonially eating octopus, for example, would cause the sickness to flee (he'e) or spread out (mahola); taro or kalo is the symbol of man and the family of the Hawaiian race, eating poi made from taro reaffirms one's Hawaiian identity. "Limu kala (seaweed) symbolically unbound or loosened man from wrong doings and mutual hostilities that marred human and human-with-god relationships" (Pūku'i, Haertig, and Lee, *Nānā I Ke Kumu* [*Look to the Source*], Vol. I, 1979, p. 2).

The orchestration of color, shape, sex, smell, taste, and touch of all things ceremonially consumed as vegetable and meat on land and in the sea were and effectively still are elements of gaining knowledge, health, and divinity.

APPLIED PSYCHO-SUPPLEMENTATION

The effectiveness of symbolism is in the perfection of its meaning. Its image must be perceived as "excellent." The source of this book comes from the Hawaiian language and people. To apply Hawaiian symbols requires the reader to be "excellent" in the memory and associations of the Hawaiian language. For this reason, a listing of Hawaiian symbols and their meanings will not be given. That information can only be obtained through personal Hawaiian sources and study. However, for the Hawaiian reader, I have included a general guide followed by a contemporary approach to psycho-supplementation or ho'omanamana.

Following is a guide to research Hawaiian symbols and their meanings.

The chapter on ʻIgenesis gave the fundamental interpretation of the four sounds or elements of creation: Ē, Ā, Ō, Ū, and the sound or word for excellence ʻI. Study words that end with these sounds and notice their association to the meaning of that word.

Word interpretations are founded on pictures as well as sounds. Study words pragmatically, not in the abstract. The reason there are hidden meanings or kaona is because the word is associated with a picture and pictures may mean a thousand words. For example an extinct volcanic crater called *Koko Crater* on the east side of the island of Oʻahu is really named *Kohelepelepe* which literally means "vagina labia minor" (Pūkuʻi, Elbert, Moʻokini, *Place Names Of Hawaii*, 1981, p. 115). The name comes from the shape of the crater that is open on one side.

Create a name list of akuas and study their kino lau or body forms in nature. Notice all aspects of their manifestations, color, shape, sex, smell, taste, and touch. "For example, one gives a black pig, rooster, and loincloth to a shark ʻaumakua. . . . Pele receives black and red bark cloths, or black and white or striped ones. . . ." (Valerio Valeri, *Kingship and Sacrifice*, p. 45–46). The symbols for the shark ʻaumakua are all masculine, the colors red and black for the volcano goddess and ʻaumakua (family god) are symbolic of molten and cooled lava, respectively. Notice no reference to a loincloth for men, just cloth, denoting female. The akua god Kū is associated with the coconuts and ulua fish as symbolic representations of masculinity. The ulua fish is the marine equivalent of man (ulua weighed over 100 lbs. and grew to five feet in length) while coconuts are the plant counterparts of man's testicles because the coconut tree was visualized as a penis stuck into the sand.

CONTEMPORARY PSYCHO-SUPPLEMENTATION

I have demonstrated the traditional application of hoʻomanamana or what I call psycho-supplementation. The system required a listing of symbols and their meanings associated by visualization. A food counterpart that visually represented that symbol was then ceremonially eaten and confirmed "excellent" or perfect.

This system was the basis of attaining spiritual, physical, emotional, and intellectual health that is just as applicable today as it has been in the past. How may we apply ho'omanamana or psycho-supplementation today even if you do not have a cultural Hawaiian language background?

As just summarized, visualization is essential for creating and perfecting symbolic representation and is only limited to the individual who defines it. So, no matter what symbolic definition is given to an object, goal, and edible counterpart, it will be just as effective.

Whether you know it or not, the Western world has been using psycho-supplementation in various ways. Eating oysters empowers virility in a man, giving sweets to a sweetheart, and toasting with champagne are just a few contemporary uses. Even popular religions that practice the ritual of the sacrament are empowering, ho'omanamana, or psycho-supplementing by consuming the meaning of the thought desired.

A very useful and easily visualized symbol of psycho-supplementation is the symbol of the seed. In Kamālamalama, the old man tells the boy of the order of things. "The answer is everywhere in nature, of which we are a part. Like a seed or 'ano'ano that is planted in the earth, watered, it grows out of the soil ... to blossom and give birth to a new seed." The Hawaiian word for "kind, nature, character, type, likeness, resemblance, image, color, moral quality, meaning" is 'ano or 'ano'ano for seed (PE, p. 24).

Every culture has a staff of life symbology. For the Irish it is the potato, for the Oriental it is rice, the Italians have pasta which is made from eggs and grain, for the Hawaiian it is taro or kalo. Fruits and eggs are also symbolic of a seed and new life and of course so are literal seeds, such as grains and nuts.

PLANTING THE SEED

I will now introduce a model to illustrate the preparation, application (visualization and consummation), and maintenance of psycho-supplementation.

Step One: Preparation

1. Time, morning breakfast. Prepare enough time to complete this breakfast without rushing.
2. Maintain calm, quiet, and ceremonious attitude.
3. Prepare your own food.
4. Choose a seed symbol such as eggs, fruit, cereal.
5. A glass or more of water, no coffee or fruit juice unless the fruit juice will be symbolic of the seed supplement.

Step Two: Visualization

1. State an objective, for example, to obtain, add to, or omit from one's spiritual, intellectual, emotional, or physical being or realm. For instance, I want to eliminate a headache, specific pain (physical or emotional), habit, addiction, or I want to be successful in a specific task (emotional, physical, spiritual, or intellectual).
2. Perfect the image. You must see it clearly. If it is a feeling, see where it is in your body.
3. Empower the seed and place the objective into the seed. Be specific. Say, "I EMPOWER THIS SEED TO: (state your objective)."

Step Three: Consummation

1. Eat the empowered food slowly and one bite at a time.
2. Focus on the objective; feel, taste, and sense the digestion of each bite as it moves into your stomach.
3. Drink a swallow of water; again feel, taste, and sense the water flowing into your stomach. Say, "I AM NURTURING THE SEED TO (state your objective)."
4. Repeat the entire process until all the food is gone with as much water as necessary.
5. When you are done eating, pause and ask yourself, "WAS IT EXCELLENT?" (Did you focus clearly? Were there no distractions?). Answer with either, "YES, IT WAS EXCELLENT" or if

in any doubt answer honestly, "NO!" If you believe it was not excellent, don't be discouraged. You can try another day. Be patient and calm—it will work for you.

Step Four: Maintenance

1. Throughout the day, whenever you drink water, repeat the words, "I AM NURTURING THE SEED TO (state your objective)." Even if you forget to state your objective, your subconscious always remembers.
2. Do not be concerned about other meals during the day. The one psycho-supplemented meal is all that is necessary.

THIS PROCESS OF PSYCHO-SUPPLEMENTATION WILL WORK FOR YOU and YOU WILL SUCCEED AT ANY OBJECTIVE YOU SET INTO IT.

When an objective is obtained a new objective may be visualized and the process applied as many times as necessary or desired.

THE EFFECTIVENESS OF PSYCHO-SUPPLEMENTATION

How does psycho-supplementation work and how effective is it?

Psycho-supplementation means to supplement psychologically or to mentally empower an objective into the mind. The part of the mind that is supplemented is the visual and sensing part of the brain, the right side of the brain. That is why the objective is visualized and sensed. It is just a matter of maintaining, enhancing, or deleting an image of one's objective, which the mind recalls like a photograph.

How effective is the mind? Very, very effective. It will respond to any request visually set as an objective. The most remarkable evidence is in the realm of hypnosis and the studies on the placebo effect.

Following is an account by professional hypnotist and author Anita Anderson-Evangelists. The account dramatically demonstrates the command potential of the human mind over the physical body.

After being placed under hypnosis by a Dr. Gilkerson, Ms. Anderson-Evangelists was told to relax the back of her right hand and assured that she would not be bothered by anything done to it. She recounts, "At that point I recall being a little nervous about what he planned to do to my hand. I also remember thinking that I'd just better get it right! He asked me to close my eyes.

"I clearly heard him open a sterile pack for a syringe needle. I felt the pressure of the needle against the skin of my right hand, then felt it slip effortlessly under the skin surface and out again about an inch away. I heard members of the class gasp and walk over for a closer look. It didn't hurt in the least, though I did feel a kind of pressure. Mostly, I was amazed that it worked so well!

"Dr. Gilkerson then asked me to choose 'one side or the other'—the entry or exit holes—for my hand to bleed from. With a kind of mental shrug, I picked the innermost puncture, not knowing exactly how I would fulfill that suggestion. When he removed the needle, the puncture I'd chosen did bleed: one long stream which I felt drip down my hand. It stopped when he said it was sufficient!" (Anita Anderson-Evangelista, *Hypnosis, A Journey into the Mind*, p. 42–43.)

Note her statement, "I also remember thinking that I'd just better get it right!" and the similarity of our process of asking "Was it excellent?"

As remarkable as this account is, it is not as readily obtained in the conscious state. The process of psycho-supplementation more closely resembles the process of post-hypnotic suggestion (but without the formal induced hypnotic state) and is reinforced simply by eating and drinking water. In either case, it is still the power of the mind.

Another remarkable ability of the mind is the placebo effect—the ability of nonmedicinal agents, such as sugar pills, to effectively mimic active medicinal drugs psychologically.

A study by Swedish researchers of 159 chronic sufferers of indigestion found that a common antacid formula relieved pain no better than a placebo, a pill containing no medicine. Even a prescription drug that blocks production of stomach acid did not relieve pain better than the placebo (*Science*, May 1986, p. 6). The effective rate of relief was measured at "roughly 25 percent." Out of 159 patients, the placebo worked 25 percent of the time overall.

Note that the placebo was taken orally and it has been suggested that the effectiveness of placebos is related to a belief system that lowers stress.

Studies also show that placebos work on very subtle levels. Studies were conducted administering placebos to subjects by a person in an adjacent room to control expectations of the outcome. Suggesting that placebos work by visual or auditory cues, "Jon D. Levine and Newton C. Gordon of the University of California at San Francisco report, however, that open and hidden doses of placebo reduce pain equally well" (*Science News*, January 12, 1985, p. 25).

The study by Jon D. Levine concludes, "More important, he adds, this experimental approach shows that subtle cues can elicit a pain-killing reaction even when the subjects cannot see the people administering the placebo. The cues are so subtle that subjects and experimenters are often not consciously aware of them, observes Levine" (ibid., p. 25).

This report further supports another detail of the power of the mind: that the mind perceives by total sensory perception. In other words, the mind is receiving and processing information that we are not even aware of 24 hours a day, every year of our lives. The subjects in the study were able to perceive a belief response without even being aware of it. Some reports suggest that placebos are effective about 25 percent of the time. That means that the human mind can initiate positive responses at least 25 percent of the time, no matter what the objective may be.

It has been calculated that chance has an effective rate of 20 percent. It has been established that anyone registering a chance rate over 20 percent is considered to have extra sensory perception or ESP. If the mind can accomplish any belief objective at least 25 percent of the time, as in the placebo effect, then is it possible to presume that the human mind can accomplish any belief objective effectively? In other words, the mind will render an answer to any question put to it consciously or subconsciously, whether the premise is true or not, correctly and with detail at least 25 percent of the time, based on this calculation of total memory and senses. Could this be the mechanism behind telepathy, clairvoyance, precognition, past lives regression, astro-projection, or trans-channeling at least 25 percent of the time? The answer in my opinion is yes. Rather than calling it extra sensory perception, it could be called *total sensory perception*.

SUMMARY TO PSYCHO-SUPPLEMENTATION

This chapter has addressed the traditions and contemporary definition, approach, and effectiveness of hoʻomanamana or what I call psycho-supplementation. I have given a model of this system for contemporary consideration and use by Hawaiian and non-Hawaiian alike.

I have presented the seed symbology as an introductory model. However, the effectiveness of this one model is unlimited by the imagination. The mastering of the seed model is only a beginning, leading to other forms and combinations of psycho-supplementation, such as by scent, sound, touch, and eventually by pure imagery and power of the mind.

The effectiveness of psycho-supplementation as in the placebo effect has been demonstrated to be at least 25 percent. It isn't hard to realize the potential of adding this system to physical supplementation as in vitamins, drugs, nutrition and psychology.

The potential of intellectual, spiritual, and emotional goals can all be supplemented by this system.

As proclaimed in our story of Kamālamalama, to all who would ask the question, the answer is yours, "You are with oiaʻiʻo or the truth."

Chapter Six

PAHU: THE LEGEND OF THE DRUM

INTRODUCTION

Pahu, The Legend of the Drum, is an observation of present-day cultures, their relations, understanding, and misunderstanding of their identity.

This story concerns three college students, in their third year at the University of Hawai'i. It melds together the relationship of three ethnic identities: Japanese, Hawaiian, and American.

Their journey into the realm of Hawaiian mysticism, symbology, nature, caring, and personal identity are the threads from which this story's tapestry is woven.

Drawing from our previous chapters, we find the universal question of identity addressed once again and mystically answered in the Hawaiian way of asking, "Mai hea mai 'oe?" "Where are you from?" By connecting one's self to an ethnic origin, the answer to who we are and where we are going can be realized. And from this base, one's ethnic values may be pursued to the universal truth or source that all thoughtful cultures possess. From these universal truths, we may honor, respect, and be considerate of one another. We all have a place in the scheme of nature.

Our story's ethnic Japanese, Tosh, is firm in his identity and relationship to Americans and Hawaiians. Kekoa is a modern-day Hawaiian who is searching for his identity but afraid to discuss it with his companions for fear of being labeled an activist and then losing their friendship. Bob is the American who came to Hawaii because it's beautiful and it's American, with all the amenities modern society can afford.

This story also reveals the intricate use of dream implantation, initiated by the *kahuna* guardian, in Kekoa's first meeting with Mr. Kahukāne, whose name means male guardian. Mr. Kahukāne admonishes, "One may hear the truth and you may see the truth, but to know the truth is to live it." This subconscious message will inspire Kekoa on a journey that will methodically and increasingly involve his own two companions, as well.

In the end, all three will be enlightened in their journey; learning the way to self-identity and understanding of one another.

The details contained in this story are based on actual natural localities, electrical phenomenon, and relics of Hawaiian origin and applications. The actual artifacts and location of the cave in this story is a composite of various localities. They are not secret and may be experienced with some inquiry and research.

PAHU: THE LEGEND OF THE DRUM
FRIDAY AFTERNOON

The story begins on a Friday and Kekoa is in one of his classes on Hawaiian religion, mythology, and ritual. His professor has invited a Hawaiian kupuna, or elder, Mr. Kahukāne, to speak on Hawaiian mythology. One of the highlights is "The Legend of the Pahu-drum."

The kupuna tells the class, "Our ancestors have told us that on special nights, if one listens, you can hear the beating of a Pahu-drum, its origin emanating from beyond our understanding. Where or how this drum is sounded no one knows. Some believe it comes from our 'aumā kua, our revered ancestors who have passed on into Pō the spirit world."

Kekoa asks the kupuna, "Sounds like a fascinating story but you can't possibly believe there's any truth to it?" The kupuna answers, "We believe these stories are based on what is, if you want to know if they are true or not, you must experience it for yourself." The kupuna adds, "You may hear the truth and you may see the truth, but to know the truth is to live it."

With that last statement, the professor thanks his guest speaker and reminds the class that their assignments will be due the following Monday. With a big smile he says, "Aloha!" Turning to Mr. Kahukāne, the professor thanks him once again with a handshake and a hug.

While the professor is thanking Mr. Kahukāne, Kekoa meets his two friends just outside the classroom door.

"How'z it? Ready to go out for pizza?" asks Bob, Kekoa's haole (Caucasian) friend.

"Yea, I'm hungry after my last exam," adds Tosh, their local Japanese companion.

"Hey, by the way, are you guys still game to go hiking Manoa Falls tomorrow?" inquires Kekoa. His two friends reply in the affirmative and head on to their favorite pizza parlor, eyeing some girls as they go.

AT THE PIZZA PARLOR

This next scene typically shows the contemporary relationship among these three ethnic identities using proper and pidgin English to express themselves and not ever expressing their personal cultural feelings. In this way, they discuss their week of studies, girls, and sports.

Over another mug of beer and a few leftover slices of pizza, Bob turns to Kekoa and asks, "Who was that guy speaking in your class today? We heard the answer he gave you at the end there. That *kahuna* stuff is pretty spooky to me."

"That was Mr. Kahukāne, a Hawaiian kupuna, elder, speaking about the legend of the Pahu-drum. You guys wouldn't believe it either," says Kekoa.

"Spooky stuff, you Hawaiians," concludes Tosh.

They all give a laugh and finally leave the pizza parlor.

SATURDAY

The next morning Kekoa awakens to the sound of his radio alarm announcing, "It's a beautiful day in Paradise and for you star-gazers a new moon this coming Tuesday." Kekoa calls up his two friends and tells them his girlfriend is going to drop them off at Paradise Park and pick them up at 5:00 p.m. after they hike up Manoa cliffs trail, via Manoa Falls.

After picking up Kekoa's two friends, Leilani, Kekoa's girlfriend drives them to the parking lot of Paradise Park at the end of Manoa valley and the guys step out.

"It's a beautiful day alright. Just like the radio said," Kekoa tells the other guys as they get out of his girlfriend's car.

"I hope you brought your own water and flashlight this time, Bob," Kekoa jokingly tells Bob.

"You better believe it. I'm prepared for anything, hunting knife, extra batteries and all."

"Now that's what I call 'Gung ho,'" laughs Tosh.

"Mahalo, my love. See you later," Kekoa tells his girlfriend as she begins to drive away.

"Well, let's go," Kekoa commands.

They wind their way up the paved road, pass the park and the arboretum, finally stepping over a log marking the beginning of their trek up to Manoa Falls. They pass over a small, well-shaded bridge spanning a small stream, then step out into a lush green setting canopied by blue sky and sculptured peaks—what most people would consider paradise.

Accompanied by the ever-present songs of forest birds, they continue hiking their way past a grove of swamp mahogany, mountain apple, and guava trees, then turn left past a forest of bamboo.

Approaching the falls, they notice a few green and brown ti leaf bundles.

Kekoa tells his friends, "Those are hoʻokupu's. There's just a stone in most of them. They're memorial gifts, out of respect for the waterfall just ahead."

“Respect for what?” asks Bob.

“I’ll tell you when we get to the falls,” replies Kekoa.

Shortly thereafter, they finally reach the falls.

“Remember the ti leaf bundles, Bob?” Kekoa asks, stepping up to the falls that are flowing with a good amount of rainfall. “It’s because this waterfall is sacred to our Hawaiian akua god Kāne.” Kekoa stands on a boulder with his hiking stick in hand and begins to reenact the story of the gods Kāne and Kanaloa seeking out awa plants for ceremonial drink.

“The god Kāne decides that this would be a good spot to plant ‘awa,” Kekoa begins, “he then raises his staff and strikes the side of the cliff before him and clears a space where the face of the mountain had stood. Then from above, a broad ribbon of sacred water begins to flow as a crystal pool before his feet, full of life and sustenance for their sacred ‘awa and thirsty valley below. Behold the waters of Kāne,” Kekoa dramatically announces.

“Wow! You should be in the movies,” Tosh slurs out.

“All right, we’ll take a break here then move on up to the left there and begin our hike up the Manoa cliffs trail,” Kekoa continues.

“This trail better be everything you said it is,” Tosh demands.

“You guys wanna quit?” Kekoa dares.

“Hell no!” snaps Bob.

“OK, ten minutes and we’re on our way,” Kekoa says while looking at his watch.

“Alright, break’s over. Let’s go,” Kekoa tells his friends. Kekoa leads the way, followed by Bob and Tosh. While partly up the trail, Bob decides to relieve himself in the bushes off the side of the trail. He yells out to the other two, “I’ll catch up. I have to take a leak.”

Stepping off the trail Bob relieves himself with a sigh and while zipping up his fly, hears some rustling in the brush. Unexpectedly, a wild boar rushes out just a few feet from him, then crosses the trail and quickly disappears, it’s grunting fading into the forest below.

Gathering his composure, Bob curiously turns and carefully steps in the direction where the wild boar had originally appeared. Snooping around, he discovers a cave behind some thick underbrush where the pig probably had a den. Bob rushes up the trail and yells out to his companions to wait up and come and see what he has found.

Gathering around the cave entrance, they clear some of the lush greenery covering the entryway. Bob pulls out his flashlight and says, "Let me go in first. Make sure you tell me if that wild boar comes back."

Crawling into a good size cave, almost big enough to stand up in and now partly lit by the outside sunlight, Bob excitedly announces to his friends outside the cave, "Take a look at this."

Kekoa and Tosh enter the cave to discover, along with Bob, a canoe and skeletal remains. Kekoa volunteers an explanation, "This must be a burial cave, common to Hawaiian ali'i, chiefs."

"This far up the mountain?" Tosh curiously asks.

"Yea. Their bones have special mana and were hidden very secretly," Kekoa explains.

"Well, it's no secret now. Hey take a look," Bob tells his two friends, pointing his flashlight to the back of the cave. "It goes on some more."

"I've heard of lava tubes like this going on for miles on the big island," Kekoa adds.

"Well let's take a look," Bob eagerly declares.

"Wait a minute, Leilani's supposed to pick us up at the end of our hike," Kekoa worriedly explains.

"Aw, we have some time, come on, just a little bit?" Bob asks. Kekoa gives in and they begin to go further into the cave.

Stepping carefully into the back of the cave, the trio begins to explore a curiosity greater than they have ever known before. Leaving the security of daylight fading behind them, they go on.

Suddenly, Tosh breaks through the cave floor and falls with a howl and a thud. Bob and Kekoa turn around in fright to find Tosh missing. Looking down with his flashlight, Bob realizes the predicament Tosh has fallen into.

Calling down into the pit, Bob and Kekoa are relieved after a short silence, by Tosh's voice saying, "I'm alright, but I think I sprained my ankle." Bob shines his flashlight down the shaft, about eight feet below, they illuminate the face of their friend staring up at them, sitting on the cave floor below.

Bob and Kekoa easily climb down the shaft to help Tosh out. Making it down the shaft, Bob asks Tosh if he can make it out. Tosh thinks he can. Then Bob curiously shining his light around, notices the cave moving further on into the distance.

"Let's get out of here! Tosh needs some help," Kekoa reminds Bob.

"Yea, you're right. Come on, lets get out of this mess," Bob commands.

Just as they begin to lift Tosh up from the floor of the cave, a large boulder falls into the shaft blocking any possibility of escape.

"Oh no, what do we do now?" yells Tosh.

"Well, at least it hasn't blocked the entire entrance. We still have lots of air and some light from the cave entrance," Bob encouragingly tells Tosh.

"Yes Tosh, when we don't show up at the end of our hike, Leilani will know something's wrong and will send help. We probably may have to spend the night though," Kekoa confidently tells himself and his companions.

"It's a good thing this didn't happen further in the cave we might never have had a chance of being found," Bob realizes.

"We'll, we're stuck here now," Tosh adds.

In their cramped predicament, but still partly lit by some light from above, Bob tells his friends he'll explore ahead to see if there is a better place to spend the night. Stepping into the darkness, Bob returns shortly to announce that the cave opens up into a large cavern, just ahead, where they may spend a more comfortable night. Bob and Kekoa gather some timber that fell in with Tosh and make a small fire in the cavern Bob has found and return to help Tosh to their temporary campsite.

"How's your foot?" asks Kekoa.

"Not too bad, I can still walk but it's very sore," replies Tosh, limping along to the fireplace.

A NIGHT IN THE CAVE

While seated around the fire, with shadows dancing around the cave, Tosh begins to get angry about the predicament he has gotten himself into. Partly because of the pain in his ankle, Tosh begins to argue with his companions. "If I hadn't listened to you guys, I wouldn't be stuck here in this rock."

"Listen, Tosh, nobody dragged you along," Kekoa snaps back.

"Why don't you shut up? You Hawaiians are always complaining, 'this is my island, this is my land, my mountain, my ocean.' Well I live here, too," Tosh frustratingly tells Kekoa.

"And you haoles, you think you own everything and do anything you want," Tosh tells Bob sarcastically.

Bob angrily retorts, "You Japs are damn lucky we didn't bomb Japan off the face of the map for what you did to us at Pearl Harbor."

A free-for-all argument ensues. Then Kekoa breaks in with a commanding voice, "What the hell are we fighting about? We're friends, remember? Hawai'i's a melting pot."

"The hell with the melting pot, I'm still Japanese, you're still Hawaiian, and he's a haole who doesn't know who the hell he is," Tosh finally concludes.

Startled by Tosh's statement, Bob yells out, "What do you mean, I don't know who I am? I'm American remember. Just like you guys."

"That's the problem. Kekoa and I are not just Americans. Yea, we're U.S. citizens under U.S. sovereignty, but I'm Japanese and proud of it. I know where I come from," Tosh tells Bob.

"And for you, Kekoa, our people know this is your ancestral land, and believe it or not, have great respect for it. Why do you think you don't hear us complaining so much?" Tosh explains to Kekoa.

Calming down, Kekoa thoughtfully replies. "You know we've studied together, we've played together, we've laughed together, but we've never ever talked to each other like this before."

"Maybe it's because you can't talk about stuff like this over pizza, booze, and women," Bob jokingly breaks in.

Sharing a laugh together, Tosh apologizes, "Yea! I'm sorry guys. I can't believe I said the things I did. We should have had this kind of talk a long time ago. Are we still friends?" asks Tosh reaching out his hand. Bob and Kekoa agree and join hands one on top of another and join in a pact of renewed friendship.

Bob decides to light up a joint and offers the pakalolo to Kekoa, who turns it down by saying, "Somebody should stay alert, in case something happens or somebody finds us. Thanks, anyway."

Bob offers it to Tosh and adds, "This will loosen you up."

Tosh takes a puff and they all settle down around the fire. After a while, Bob and Tosh are fast asleep leaving Kekoa to watch over them.

Kekoa studies the shadows dancing around the cave while the fire crackles quietly before him. Then suddenly Kekoa is startled at the sound of an owl. Shining his flashlight in the direction of the sound, Kekoa gets up and carefully moves to the far end of the cave. He discovers that the cave continues down still further. Still within sight of the fire, Kekoa steps into the passageway and no sooner has he moved three feet when the owl he heard is staring him right in the eyes. Simultaneously, the owl gives out a cry and Kekoa jerks back and drops the flashlight. Quickly reaching down and finding it, he stands up and shines the light at the ledge where the owl had just stood seconds ago, but is surprised to see that it is not there. With a big sigh, Kekoa returns to the campfire and finds his two companions still fast asleep.

THE DREAM

Kekoa settles down and in a moment begins to nod out, only to be abruptly brought to consciousness by Bob suddenly perking up into a sitting position, wide eyed, asking Kekoa if he had said something, "Huh, what did you say?"

"Say what? I didn't say a word. I was almost fast asleep," replies Kekoa.

"Wow, I really thought I heard someone say, as clear as I'm talking to you, 'Where are you from?'"

"It was just a dream," Kekoa confidently tells Bob. Assured it was just a dream, Bob turns on his side and soon is back asleep.

Kekoa returns to the sounds of the fire and quiet breathing of his companions. An hour goes by when suddenly and by surprise both of his companions bolt from their sleep and in a ricochet fashion, call out to Kekoa, "What did you say?"

Rushing back from the back of the cave, Kekoa asks, "What's going on here? Don't tell me you both are having the same dream? Come on!" Kekoa doubtfully tells his friends.

"I heard it again," says Bob.

"Heard what?" Tosh questions Bob.

Bob turns to Tosh and says, "I thought I heard someone ask me, 'Where are you from?'"

"That's what I heard," Tosh confusingly reveals.

"Hell no, it was that pakalolo you guys had," Kekoa tells Bob and Tosh.

"You mean you didn't hear anything?" Tosh asks Kekoa. "Man, what a night. The only thing I heard while you two where asleep was an owl," Kekoa tells his friends. Pointing the flashlight to the back of the cave, Kekoa continues, "I followed the sound a few steps down a passage way there and the bird almost scared the heck out of me when I found him on a ledge staring me right in the face."

"Is it still there?" Bob asks.

"No, he must have flown away after I dropped the flashlight. Funny though, I didn't hear it fly away," Kekoa curiously replies.

Wide awake now, Bob gets his flashlight and goes to the end of the cave where Kekoa saw the owl and discovers something. Bob calls Kekoa over and points to the floor of the passage way and asks Kekoa, "I thought you said you only went this far."

"I did," says Kekoa.

"Then how come your footprints continue on into the tunnel?" Bob asks Kekoa.

"Those are not my footprints, I'm wearing shoes. Those prints are a couple of bare feet," Kekoa explains.

Staring at one another, Bob surmises, "These footprints must be of some ancient Hawaiian." Kekoa agrees. "Maybe they lead out of here. Let's follow them," Bob tells Kekoa. "Let's tell Tosh," Kekoa adds.

Returning back to the fire, Bob and Kekoa tell Tosh that they might be able to find another way out.

They tell Tosh to stay put but Tosh anxiously declares, "No way am I staying here alone. I'm going with you."

"OK. Let's go, but leave the fire burning, so we can find our way back," says Kekoa.

THE HEIAU

The trio begins to follow the narrow passageway, guided by the possibilities that the ancient footprints might lead to a way out of the cave. Then, illuminated by their flashlight, Kekoa notices some drawings carved into the rock wall.

"Petroglyphs, hundreds of them; they're covering the whole passageway," Kekoa excitedly points out to Bob and Tosh. Then, almost without notice, they enter a large chamber, practically stumbling over one another as they do so. Pointing their flashlight about the chamber, they glimpse four massive akua tiki images from what seems to be a full-scale Hawaiian temple.

"I don't believe it," says Kekoa.

"This is fantastic," Bob adds with excitement.

"OK, this looks really cool guys, but remember we're supposed to be finding a way out?" Tosh reminds his friends.

"Where's the way out? This is probably the greatest find in recent history and all you can think of is 'Where's the way out?'" Kekoa tells Tosh.

"Don't worry, Tosh, we'll find it," Says Bob.

"Hey we better take some pictures," Bob tells Kekoa.

"With what?" replies Kekoa. They both look at Tosh and he replies, "Don't look at me—I don't have one."

Finding some timber from the site, they build another fire that finally reveals the awesome dimensions of their discovery. Lit in eerie detail, Kekoa recognizes a raised altar platform, white coral-covered terraces, a full-height temple tower, and two thatched houses designed with no windows and one frontal entrance. Kekoa points to one of thatched structures and says, "One of these must be the mana house, where sacred objects were cared for. The other one must be the Pahu-drum house. I think this is the mana house from the layout of this heiau temple."

With Bob standing to the left of the entrance to the mana house, Kekoa volunteers to go in first. Bending low, Kekoa creeps in and illuminates a disappointing empty structure. "What do you see?" Bob anxiously asks Kekoa.

"Four walls and nothing in between," Kekoa answers, crawling back out.

"You mean there's nothing in there?" Bob asks Kekoa.

"No. The objects must have been moved for some reason," Kekoa answers Bob.

THE SECRET OF THE DRUM

At that moment, a loud drum beat echoes through the cavern. "Boom!" Stunned, the three adventurers stand frozen in disbelief.

"That can't be," whispers Kekoa. "Boom!" Another drum beat.

"Listen, we better get out of here," Tosh tells the others.

"Wait a minute, you don't see anybody coming after us do you?" Bob tells Kekoa and Tosh.

"Yea, you're right," Tosh replies.

"Listen. The sound's coming from that structure over there. What did you say that was, Kekoa?" Bob asks.

"The Pahu-drum house," replies Kekoa.

"That figures, but who's beating the drum?" Tosh adds.

"Well, here's our chance to find out," Bob daringly challenges.

This time, Bob leads the way. With his two companions following close behind, they quietly creep up to the entrance of the hut. Mustering his courage, Bob grits his teeth and carefully peeks into the hut.

"I don't see anything," says Bob in a whisper.

"Well, shine your light," Kekoa tells Bob.

"Well, here goes," Bob says while flicking on his flashlight.

To their astonishment, they find no one in the hut and, looking at one another, Tosh tells his friends, "Now this is too much. Let's get out of here!"

Then, before their very eyes, while peering into the shack, they hear another drum beat, again from the empty hut. "Boom!"

"Look there," Bob excitedly tells his friend.

Looking at the floor of the hut, they see an opening. Gently pushing Bob aside, Kekoa courageously says, "I'm gonna find out about this once and for all," and enters the shack with Bob right behind.

"Stay outside Tosh and keep a lookout," Bob tells Tosh.

Inside the shack, they find a passageway leading down farther into the cave. Winding their way for a few minutes they finally enter a small chamber. "Boom!" And the two explorers are practically knocked to the floor of the cave. Holding on to the rocky walls for support, their light reveals a small pool of water.

Then, Kekoa senses something. "You smell that, Bob? Smells like salt air from the sea." Kekoa kneels beside the pool and tastes the water.

Surprisingly, Kekoa tells Bob, "But this is spring water, it's not salty at all!"

"So, where's the sea smell coming from?" asks Bob.

"Listen!" Kekoa commands in a whisper. "Do you hear what I hear?" Kekoa asks Bob.

"It sounds like the sea," Bob answers.

"Look over there, above that ledge," Kekoa tells Bob.

Shining their flashlight, they reveal a small oval opening about two feet wide. "We are hearing the ocean. And that booming sound must be some type of wave crashing into the opening of this lava tube, somewhere on our shoreline," Kekoa logically concludes.

"So this is the legend of the drum," Bob tells Kekoa.

"Well, I'll be," exclaims Kekoa.

"Let's get back to Tosh and tell him what we've found," Bob excitedly tells Kekoa.

A GUARDIAN'S SECRET

Rushing back from their discovery, up the passageway from the spring, and out of the hut, Kekoa and Bob find Tosh missing.

"Where did he go? He couldn't have gone back to the cave entrance," Bob confusingly tells Kekoa.

"Look here, Bob," Kekoa points to some footprints on the cave floor leading to the back of the temple site.

"Hey, they're more than just his footprints. There are those old Hawaiian tracks again. It's leading up this passageway. Tosh might have found a way out," Kekoa tells Bob.

"Well, let's go," Bob eagerly commands.

The tunnel narrows till the two have to bend down and enter another wider opening. And there sprawled out on the floor, half dazed is Tosh.

"Are you all right?" Bob asks Tosh, reaching down to help him.

"Yea, I'm OK, I must have bumped my head on that ledge coming in here," Tosh assures his companions. Kekoa then yells out to the other two.

"Will you look at this?" pointing his flashlight to the center of the room. And there, placed upon a stone altar before them, is a beautifully colored, feather akua image. Small enough to be carried in one's arms, colored in red, yellow, and black. Its mouth ringed in teeth and eyes seemingly glaring out for the intrusion that these three have made on its secret hiding place. "This image must have originally been in the mana house at the temple site. Its guardian must have placed it here a long time ago, as it's final resting place," Kekoa explains.

"Hey, do you feel something strange?" Tosh asks his friends.

"Yea, the hair on the back of my neck is beginning to tingle," says Kekoa.

"Look at this. The hair on my arms is standing up," Bob shows his friends.

Then, turning to the akua figure, they notice the feathers fluttering and rising. Sparks begin to crackle with a blue light between the layers of bird feathers. And then from its mouth an eerie sound begins to emanate, echoing through the cave. Frightened, the trio steps back and the sound begins to get louder. A blue aura engulfs the figure illuminating the entire chamber of the cave, revealing petroglyphs covering every inch of the walls and ceiling. Suddenly long crooked blue lines of electricity flash out at the trio, dancing about in flashes of blue and violet, crackling with excitement.

Terrified, the trio scrambles out of the chamber, Tosh stumbling as they try as fast as they can to get away from what might happen next.

Entering the temple site with their campfire still burning, the ground begins to tremble and a terrible roaring sound fills the room. Rocks begin to fall from the sides of the cavern. The guys continue running, trying to remember the direction from which they originally came.

With Bob leading the way, Tosh behind him, and Kekoa at the rear, they move as fast as their fears will carry them, followed by the crashing and bellowing of rock and dirt, just at their heels.

"We've got to make it to the entrance," Bob cries out, as they finally reach the end of the tunnel. Piling up on one another, expecting the end to come, the rumbling stops.

Clearing from the dust and settling rocks, they find all but their exit covered in rocks and dirt. Out of breath and sprawled out on the floor of the cave, Kekoa, Tosh, and Bob take toll of their condition and predicament.

"Are you guys alright?" Kekoa finally calls out to his friends.

"Yea, I think so," Bob replies.

"How's your ankle?" Kekoa asks Tosh.

"It hurts like hell, but I think I'm gonna make it."

"Well, thank goodness we're still alive. Well, we've got no choice now but to wait till they find us tomorrow," Kekoa tells his friends. Totally exhausted, the three companions finally fall asleep.

THE NEXT DAY

Morning has come once again to the valley and from below the shaft our trio awakens to the call of a rescue team just outside the cave entrance.

"We're here," Bob, Kekoa, and Tosh call out in unison, again and again.

Soon Kekoa hears a familiar voice calling from above.

"Are you alright, Kekoa?" Kekoa's girlfriend, Leilani, urgently asks.

"Yea, we're OK!" Kekoa replies. Soon the boulder blocking the shaft is cleared by a team of rescue workers and all three are safe at last.

"Wow. What a find," says one of the rescue team.

"You've found a Hawaiian burial cave totally intact. The museum will be happy to hear about this one," he adds. Recalling their adventure and the loss of every clue of what they had really found, the three friends look at one another with regret and think to themselves, *if they only knew!* Except for Tosh's sprained ankle, all three weathered their incredible experience very well and are released from the hospital emergency room to be reunited with their concerned family members.

THE MEANING OF TRUTH

The following night, the three friends join one another at Kekoa's home in Manoa and recollect their experience the night before.

"How's your foot, Tosh?" asks Bob.

"Oh, it'll have to be bandaged for a while but, otherwise, glad to be alive," replies Tosh.

"We didn't get a chance to tell you, Tosh, but we found out where the drum sounds were coming from," Kekoa tells Tosh.

"Yea. It was coming from the crashing of ocean waves in some lava tube echoing all the way from some shoreline," Bob authoritatively explains.

"No supernatural beings?" Tosh asks.

"I'm afraid not," Kekoa tells Tosh, shaking his head slowly.

Then Bob questions Kekoa, "What about those footprints? How do you explain that they never did lead out of the cave."

"That's something we'll never know," Kekoa answers. "By the way, Tosh, thanks for sharing your feelings with us. I didn't realize how important it was to hear that from you," Kekoa reveals to Tosh.

"You know what?" Bob begins to tell his friends, "in spite of almost getting killed, I feel a hell of a lot different. I really can't explain it but the things you said, Tosh, and that dream I had asking me where am I from, got me to really thinking. You're right, Tosh, I've never given thought to where I come from, as far as racial pride and identity goes. My mom says I'm Irish, German, English and some American Indian. And now that I think of it, she was pretty proud of her Indian ancestry. Natchez, I think. I'm gonna really check into it. What about you, Kekoa?" Bob asks.

At that very instant they hear the hoot of an owl just outside their patio lanai. Rushing out and overlooking a street below, they all catch the flight of a white owl sailing down and under the light of an amber street light, gliding effortlessly up and back into the darkness of the valley.

Staring at one another, Kekoa says in disbelief, "No, it couldn't be."

"Come on, Kekoa, none of that spooky stuff again," Bob tells Kekoa as he and Tosh go back into the house.

While Kekoa stares up into the valley, he glimpses, once again, the owl gliding back into the glow of the street lamp as if to say goodbye. Recalling the words of the kupuna, elder, Kekoa says, "Mahalo, thank you, my kupuna. I now have lived the truth."

Chapter Seven

ALOHA: THE HAWAIIAN WAY TO LOVE

No other word in the Hawaiian language has been so thoroughly interpreted and used so freely than the word aloha.

The definition of aloha can be found in any standard English and Hawaiian dictionary and is generally interpreted to mean love. As simple as the definition may seem, the definition of love seems to be the elusive word in question. Ask anyone the meaning of love and you'll get as many interpretations of love as you will of aloha.

The simplicity of the meaning of love as aloha is not in the definition of the words but in living it. By demonstrating the Hawaiian way to love we can understand the Hawaiian way of aloha.

THE LIVING EXPRESSION OF ALOHA

My first memory of aloha came as a young boy observing the manner in which my ancestors would express themselves when meeting. Seeing one another in the distance, they would call out in long breaths, affectionately to one another, "You there!" "Ui, eia nei!" And the host would call out, "Aloha mai!" "Come, come, come!" Gradually building to an emotional pitch, with eyes moistened with joy and fixed on one another, they would embrace, touching nose to cheek, expressing their feelings of aloha. This exchange of embrace and touching face to face was repeated when leaving as well.

Experiencing this would make sense of the components of the word aloha: Alo meaning face and ha meaning to breathe. To breathe upon the face. How else would one show, so intimately, that he or she cared than by touching face to face.

THE DUALISM OF LOVE

The dualism of love between husband and wife means the emotional or romantic and sexual expression of love.

In the book, *Nānā I Ke Kumu*, Hawaiian historian Mary Kawena Pūkuʻi was asked to speak on "the deep love of man and woman." The previous chapter had just discussed "sexual expression" and Kawena replied, "You mean it is time to put together what belongs together" (Pūkuʻi, Haertig, Lee, and McDermott, *Nānā I Ke Kumu*, Vol. II, p. 114).

The celebration of life is the Hawaiian way of life. To pursue in all things a level of excellence is the mark of one beloved. The living of aloha by caring and touching is paralleled by romance and making love to its highest level and this is the Hawaiian ideal. The dualism of love is one in aloha.

These ideals are poetically expressed in the philosophy of our songs and chants to celebrate life. One's beauty is likened as a rare flower in the highest place, sought after by so many birds.

And passion is expressed as "moving waters of desire."

THE PURPOSE OF ALOHA

The joys and pleasures of love as aloha have a very real purpose in Hawaiian life. This celebration of love at its highest level of excellence blossoms in the foundation of a family, the cornerstone of Hawaiian culture.

All children are beloved as blossoms, the flowers, na pua, of Hawaiʻi. "He lei poina ʻole ke keiki." "A lei (garland) never forgotten is the beloved child" (Pūkuʻi, *ʻOlelo Noʻeau*, verse 740, p. 82).

Even in the case of a childless union, the free exchange of charity by a family blessed with many children is practiced by the literal giving of one's own to another. All children are beloved as blossoms of the union of romantic and sexual love, of aloha. What greater love than to literally give the blossoms of one's love to another?

EVERLASTING LOVE

The nurturing of love as aloha between husband and wife is perpetuated in the blossoms of their union, their children, who in turn carry on the ideals of aloha as demonstrated by their ancestors and practiced in their own lives. Love is everlasting.

"E lei kau, e lei ho'oilo i ke aloha." "Love is worn like a wreath through the summers and the winters" (Pūku'i, *'Olelo No'eau*, verse 332, p. 40).

ALOHA 'OE

I have shown that the living expression aloha is love and that the dualism of romantic and sexual love are one and of the highest ideal. That by pursuing love as aloha at its highest level of excellence is a celebration of life, and from its union comes the blossoms of everlasting love, a family, a new generation of aloha.

Touching and caring as a friend, lover, and family is the natural and Hawaiian way to love. Aloha.

FOOTNOTE

This essay was written in 1988 and was later published as a Christmas message of aloha in the Office of Hawaiian Affairs newspaper, *Ka Wai Ola O Oha*, December 1990. The essay was also included in my book, *The Need for Hawai'i–A Guide to Hawaiian Cultural and Kahuna Values*, published in 1991.

CONCLUSION

Every word, vision, and experience in this book has been my personal journey to knowledge, truth, and enlightenment. They are only a part of a continuing and enormously rewarding pursuit of life.

Sharing this with others declares that the knowledge of our honored ancestors is not lost. Some traditions may have been forgotten, but the source of our kūpuna (grandparents) and *kahuna* (Hawaiian religious-philosopher) is still with us today. It is all around us, in every Hawaiian name, place, gesture, color, and sound. We have only to ask the question, seek out the answer, and make the truth our own.

Where we come from is where we are going, and to live a life in honor and excellence is our pursuit in life. We are all responsible for our deeds and deeds accounted to our lives.

The principles of a Hawaiian way to learn, seek out and obtain truths, are the instruments to chant out a celebration of life, aloha, love and caring.

Knowing the basic truths of life, of who we are, where we come from, and where we are going, are the cornerstones of building confidence and purpose to approach and accomplish any task or dream.

These principles can be applied in every aspect of life, work, politics, and play.

These words have been long overdue. The seed is planted. May it be nurtured to bloom in the hearts of all thoughtful minds and continue for a new millennium: The age of the Hawaiian.

Let us be as the lehua-eating ʻoʻopu and journey to the source, e hele i ka māpunapuna. Aloha a hui hou kākou!

GLOSSARY

ahui hou Till we meet again.

ʻahuʻula Feather cloak or cape.

akua Ancestral god.

ākua Ancestral gods.

aliʻi Chief, cheifess.

alo Front, face.

aloha Love, affection.

ʻano Likeness, image.

ʻanoʻano Seed.

ʻanoʻi Desire, beloved. Lit.: Supreme likeness, image.

ao Light.

ʻaumakua Ancestral, family, or personal god.

ʻaumākua Ancestral, family, or personal gods.

Auwē! Oh! Oh, dear! Alas!

ʻehu Fifth meaning for reddish tinge in hair of Polynesians and not hair of Caucasians.

hā To breathe.

haka Third meaning for a crested feather helmet.

Haʻo To desire, hereditary chief, island, name of a star (possibly Sirius).

haole White person, Caucasian.

Hawaiian A person of native Hawaiian ancestry.

heiau Pre-Christian Hawaiian place of worship, temple.

Hina Polynesian goddess or demigoddess, frequently associated with the moon.

hula Hawaiian form of dancing.

ʻI Supreme.

Iʻa (Capitalized) Milky Way.

kāhili Feather standard, symbolic of royalty.

kahu Guardian.

kahuna Priest, minister, (modern) expert in anything.

Kanaloa One of the four major ancestral gods of Polynesia, companion to the god Kāne.

Kāne The leading ancestral god of the four major gods of Polynesia.

kāne Male, husband, man.

kaona Hidden meaning.

kapa Tapa, bark cloth.

Kekoa A Hawaiian name meaning "the warrior."

keʻokeʻo White, clear.

Kū One of the four major ancestral gods of Polynesia.

Kumulipo Name of the Hawaiian creation chant, origin, source of life.

kupuna Grandparent, ancestor.

kūpuna Grandparents, ancestors.

Laka God or goddess of the hula.

lama Endemic ebony tree (*Diospyros*), torch, light.

lehua Blossom of the lehua or ʻohiʻa tree.

lei Garland, wreath.

Leilani A Hawaiian name meaning "heavenly garland."

lipo Deep blue-black.

Lono One of the four major ancestral gods of Polynesia.

maile Twining shrub (*Alyxia olivaeformis*) used in decoration and leis.

makua Parent.

mākua Parents.

malama Light.

mālamalama Light of knowledge, enlightenment.

mana Power.

Manoa A valley located in Honolulu, Hawai'i.

māpunapuna Bubbling spring.

mo'opuna Grandchild.

niho palaoa Whale tooth, whale-tooth pendant, a symbol of royalty.

oia'i'o Truth.

'ole Not, without, lacking.

'o'opu Variety of fresh or saltwater fish (*Eleotridae* and *Gobiidae*).

pahu First definition for drum.

pau Finished, ended.

Pele The volcano goddess.

pō Night, darkness, obscurity, the realm of the gods.

poe Round, rounded.

pueo Hawaiian short-eared owl (*Asio flammeus sandwichensis*).

pūlo'ulo'u Tapa-covered ball on a stick carried before a chief to signify a taboo.

taro Kalo (*Colocasia esculenta*) a leaf and starchy root food staple baked or pounded into a paste called poi.

tī Kī plant (*Cordyline terminalis*). Slender, unbranched stem topped with narrow, oblong leaves. Colors of leaves vary from plant to plant, green being predominant for ceremony.

Ui, eia nei! Listen, you there!

wai Water, liquid of any kind.

BIBLIOGRAPHY

Anderson-Evangelista, Anita, *Hypnosis, A Journey into the Mind*, Arco Publishing, New York, 1980.

Asimov, Isaac, *Asimov on Astronomy*, Doubleday, Garden City, New York, 1974.

Astronomy, AstroMedia, Kalmbach Publishing Company, Milwaukee, 1988.

Atlas of Hawaii, second edition, University of Hawaii Press, Honolulu.

Beckwith, Martha Warren, *The* Kumulipo, *A Hawaiian Creation Chant*, University of Hawaii Press, Honolulu, 1981.

Bryan, E. H., Jr., *Stars over Hawaii*, The Petroglyph Press, Hilo, Hawaii, 1977.

Charlot, John, *Chanting the Universe, Hawaiian Religious Culture*, Emphasis International Publisher, Hong Kong, 1983.

Gutmanis, June, *Na Pule Kahiko, Ancient Hawaiian Prayers*, Editions Limited Publisher, Honolulu, 1983.

HEN, *Hawaiian Enthnographical Notes*, vols. 1–3. Typescript, Bernice Pauahi Bishop Museum Library, Honolulu.

Holy Bible, The, Containing the Old and New Testaments, King James Version, 1611, revised 1769.

Johnson, Rubellite Kawena, and John Kaipo Mahelona, *Nā Inoa Hōkū, A Catalogue of Hawaiian and Pacific Star Names*, Topgallant Publishing Company, Honolulu, 1975.

Ka'ano'i, Patrick, and Robert Lokomaika'iokalani Snakenberg, *The Hawaiian Name Book*, Bess Press, Honolulu, 1988.

Ka'ano'i, Patrick, *The Need for Hawai'i, A Guide to Hawaiian Cultural and Kahuna Values*, Ka'ano'i Productions, 1991, second edition 1992.

Malo, David, *Hawaiian Antiquities*, Bishop Museum Press, Honolulu, 1980.

Menzel, Donald H., and Jay M. Pasachoff, *A Field Guide to the Stars and Planets*, second edition, Houghton Mifflin Company, Boston, 1983.

Pacific Islands Monthly, Book Review, *The Kumulipo, A Hawaiian Creation Chant* by Martha Beckwith, 1981.

Pūku'i, Mary Kawena, *'Olelo No'eau, Hawaiian Proverbs and Poetical Sayings*, Bishop Museum Press, Honolulu, 1983.

Pūku'i, Mary Kawena, and Samuel H. Elbert, *Hawaiian Dictionary*, University of Hawaii Press, Honolulu, 1981.

Pūku'i, Mary Kawena, Samuel H. Elbert, and Esther T. Mookini, *Place Names of Hawaii*, University of Hawaii Press, Honolulu, 1981.

Pūku'i, Mary Kawena, E. W. Haertig, and Catherine A. Lee, *Nānā I Ke Kumu (Look to the Source)*, Volume I, Hui Hanai Publishing, Honolulu, 1979.

Pūku'i, Mary Kawena, E. W. Haertig, Catherine A. Lee, and John F. McDermott, Jr. M.D., *Nānā I Ke Kumu (Look to the Source)*, Volume II, The Queen Lili'uokalani Children's Center, 1979.

Reader's Digest Wide World Atlas with Rand McNally Maps, Reader's Digest Association, New York, 1981.

Reader's Digest Great Encyclopedic Dictionary, Including Funk & Wagnalls Standard College Dictionary, New York, The Readers Digest Association, 1966.

Science, May 1986.

Science News, January 12, 1985.

Steiger, Walter R., *Comet Halley Handbook*, for *Hawai‘i Observer: 1985–1986*, Special Publication No. 73, Bishop Museum Press, Honolulu, 1985.

Sterling, Elspeth P., and Catherine C. Summers, *Sites of Oahu*, Department of Anthropology, Department of Education, Bernice P. Bishop Museum, Honolulu, 1978.

Valeri, Valerio, *Kingship and Sacrifice, Ritual and Society in Ancient Hawaii*, translated by Paula Wissing, The University of Chicago Press, Chicago and London, 1985.

INDEX

I

J

K

P

R

S

T

U

V

W

Z